Stearman

Books by Martin W. Bowman:

Stearman

A Pictorial History
Jim Avis and Martin Bowman

Motorbooks International
Publishers & Wholesalers

This edition first published in 1997 by Motorbooks International Publishers & Wholesalers, 729 Prospect Avenue, PO Box 1, Osceola, WI 54020 USA.

© 1997 Martin Bowman

Previously published by Airlife Publishing Ltd, Shrewbury, England.

Motorbooks International is a certified trademark, registered with the United States Patent Office.

The information in this book is true and complete to the best of our knowledge. All recommendations are made without any guarantee on the part of the author or publisher, who also disclaim any liability incurred in connection with the use of this data or specific details.

We recognize that some words, model names and designations, for example, mentioned herein are the property of the trademark holder. We use them for identification purposes only. This is not an official publication.

Motorbooks International books are also available at discounts in bulk quantity for industrial or sales-promotional use. For details write to Special Sales Manager at the Publisher's address.

Library of Congress Cataloging-in-Publication Data Available.

ISBN 0-7603-0479-3

Printed and bound in Singapore.

Contents

Acknowledgements

A big vote of thanks goes to Bart Halter, William T. Larkins, Addison Pemberton, Gordon Plaskett and Ron and Carol Rex, who from the outset showed enthusiasm and continued to provide unstinting assistance and support throughout. William T. Larkins supplied a range of superb photographs when others denied them, and graciously contributed his detailed knowledge. He is, more than any other, responsible for ensuring that any potential gaps were filled. Credit must go to Thomas J. Fitton for unearthing the astonishing account of the Stearman in combat in the Philippines. Phil Kemp and the late Larry S. Smalley provided the majority of information for the detailed appendix section.

No less important are the contributions made, but which are too numerous and detailed to be mentioned, by the following individuals. They are listed strictly in alphabetical order as it is unfair to single out anyone from among those who submitted the 'old and new' photographs which so very beautifully feature the Stearman – their credit lines in the captions are their accolade:

Evan Adams; Bert Allam; Willis M. Allen Jr; Mabry I. Anderson; Eddie Andreini; Richard E. 'Dick' Bagg; Dave Bagshaw AFC RAF (Retd); Paul Ballance; Anthony P. Banham; Robert J. Barden Sr; F. Norman Bate MBE, Arnold Register; Jonathan Beck; Tim Beck; R.G. 'Dick' Beeler; James F. Belwood; Dennis F. and Carolyn Blankenbaker; Ed and Christine Boulter; Dick Brebner; E.J. Brown, 6 BFTS Assn; Robert H. Brown, Falcon Field Assn; Cal Butler; Bob Cameron; Robert E. Carlin; Margaret R. Carter; Earl D. Caton; Roland Chase; John Chopelas; Ken Clarkson; Al Cleave; Wilbur L. Clingan; Sue Cogswell; Ken Cranefield; Arthur Culff; Troy Culpepper; Susan D. Dacy; Richard D. Darnell; Victor Deboni; Robert V. Dickey; Graham Dinsdale; Don Downie; Danny Doyle; Bob Drake; Pearlie M. Draughn, Research Librarian, *Air Force* Magazine; Robert V. Dubay; Dusters & Sprayers Supply Inc.; Eric D. Edwards; John W. Fields; Kenneth Fields; Margie Fitzgerald, Nat Agricultural Museum; Alex Flett; Bill Frame, Airshow Manager, Eddie Andreini Airshows; the late L. James Freeman; Caroline Frick; Air Commodore Jack W. Frost; Bryan Gait; Dave Gauthier; George B. Gosney; Ron Gould; James Grover; Bryan Hamilton; Philip Handleman; Albert Hansen, Editor, AAHS Journal; Charles W. Harris, Chairman, National Biplane Assn; Chris Harrison; Bee Haydu; Pete Henry; Walter Henry, Canadian Aviation Historical Society; Peter Hoffman; Robert Holder; Gerry Honey OBE RAF (Retd); Eric Hopper; Hal Hubener, Special Collections Librarian, Lakeland Public Library, Florida; Charles Hyer; Major Enrique R. Ibárgüen; Chris Jefferson; Steve Jefferson; Bob Jesko; John Jordan; Les R. Kares; L.A. Kemp; A. Richard King; Walter J. Konantz; Dick Knapinski, Public Relations, EAA Aviation Center; Capt Reg Levy DFC; Alan Lopez, Northeast Stearman Assoc.: Tom E. Lowe; Tom Lubbesmeyer, The Boeing Co. Historical Archives; Dennis Ludwig; Eric Lundhal; Capt Bill McCash AFM, Chairman, Falcon Field Assn; Bob McComb; Lt-Col Tom H. McKiernan, USAF (Retd); Thomas L. McQuoid; R.J. McWhorter; Oak Mackey; Clem L. Maher; Bob Markow; Jerry Marlette; W.A. Marsano; Bob Meakin; Eugene A. Megas; Harry Melling; Rudolph Mick ADRC USN (Retd); John Mohr; Ken M. Molson; Bruce Monk; Col Robert K. Morgan USAF Retd; Roger Mott, Emil Buehler Naval Aviation Library; Vic Norman; John and Delia Norris; Mike O'Leary; William Mike O'Rourke; Francie Meisner Park; Robert H. Pedersen; Chester L. Peek Ph.D; Scott Perdue; Robert Peters MBE, 5 BFTS Assn; R.E. Pigney; Gordon Plaskett; Barnard C. Pollard; W. Stewart Preston; Allan Pudsey; William Reid VC; Brian F. Riggs, President, SRA; Jeff Robinson; Harry E. Rowan; Victor Salas Jr; William Ben Scott; Edwin J. Sealy; Martin and Vicky Shaw; Robert H. Sherwood; Maurice Shippey; A.J. Shortt, Director, Nat Aviation Museum, Ottawa; Michael Skeen; Southwest Airways; K. John Stableford; Don Stebbings; Richard A. Stettner; Richard Stevens; Richard A. 'Dick' Stevens; Alan H. Stredwick, 3 BFTS; Lyn Sund, Mohr Barnstorming; John Swope; Harry Tanzer; Robert L. Taylor, Antique Airplane Assoc. Inc.; Jim Temple; E.A. Thistlethwaite; Sam Tweedie; Paul Victor; John K. Vowles; Michael J. Walton; John Ware; Ray B. 'Bob' White RAF (Retd); Ron Whittaker; Dr Edward Wilkus; Nick Williams; Charles P. Wohlforth, *Alaska* Magazine; Frank E. Wolf; Tom J. Wood, Editor, Aviation AgPilot Int.; McGehee Word Jr; Richard L. Ziegler, Boeing Company.

Preface

All of us are familiar with the exploits of the WWII planes like the Mustang and Spitfire, Lancaster and Fortress, *et al.* A vast majority of pilots took their first steps towards gaining their 'wings' in the cockpit of the Stearman, among them Preddy and Bong, three Victoria Cross recipients and two American presidents. This sturdy, dependable biplane is often overlooked, yet few other aircraft in history have enjoyed such a cosmopolitan career, one which now spans eight decades of achievement. Before the war Stearmans were the sumptuous domain of the rich and famous, socialites and speedsters. C-3s, LT-1s, M-2s and Model 4s criss-crossed America, dotting the air lanes, hauling the mail. At the other end of the social scale old stagers shed their glad rags and 'dusted' corn and cotton for a living, while at country fairs itinerant barnstormers thrilled the crowds and gave humble citizens their first 'hops' around their towns. Many made up the tens of thousands of cadet pilots when 'Uncle Sam' needed them most. When in 1945 peace was resumed, Stearmans did it all again.

Finding photographs of sufficient quality with which to illustrate the seventy-year history of the Model 75 and its antecedents would therefore appear a daunting task. However, all Stearmans are held in such high esteem by legions of affectionate owners and former fliers that a veritable deluge of historical material, phone calls and letters flooded in from all over the world. There is none so unique as the amazing episode in the Philippines in 1942, which is published here for the first time. Equally, the colourful 'duster' era has been so wonderfully encapsulated by reminiscences and photos from dusters and their devotees. Thanks to the skill and determination of all the contributors, the photos which encompass the 1920s, the thirties, WWII and after feature rare pictorial essays of Stearmans in fascinating situations. It has meant that the final selection, made even more exacting because each photograph not only has to be historic but also of high quality, has been well nigh impossible.

Lloyd Carlton Stearman, one of America's great aviation pioneers. Born 26 October 1898 in Wellsford, Kansas, he died of cancer at his home in Northridge, California on 3 April 1975 aged seventy-six.

1. The Early Stearmans

Lloyd Carlton Stearman, one of America's great aviation pioneers, was born in Wellsford, Kansas, on 26 October 1898, the first of four children. His father, Fred Carlton Stearman, was a draughtsman and his mother, Icie May, was a music teacher. As a young man Lloyd's main interests were playing the violin and listening to classical music (later, at the age of fifty-eight, he carved his own violin from a single block of wood). Lloyd attended elementary and high school in Harper, Kansas and in 1917 he enrolled in the Kansas State College in Manhattan, Kansas where he studied architecture and engineering. As a teenager, he built an automobile completely from scratch. His studies were interrupted by WWI and on 21 August 1918 he enlisted in the US Navy Reserve Flying Corps as a Student Officer. At North Island Naval Air Station at San Diego, California, Stearman learned to fly in Curtiss N-9 seaplanes but on 11 November 1918 the Great War ended before he could join an operational unit.

In December 1918 Lloyd completed his studies and went to work as an architect for SS Voight and Sons, in Wichita, Kansas. Stearman soon tired of this. In 1919 he responded to an advertisement in the Wichita newspaper by Jake Moellendick and Matty Laird for an aircraft mechanic in their company. Laird was developing a three-place, open-cockpit biplane funded by Moellendick and called the 'Swallow'. Laird used the same 'stick and wire' construction as the Curtiss 'Jenny' of WWI fame. Stearman took a drop of twenty dollars a week in his salary and went to work for Moellendick and Laird building wooden wings and fuselages for Swallow aircraft. These were the first airplanes sold commercially in the United States. Despite their efforts, the Swallow was only a slight improvement over the Jenny. Stearman worked his way up, first to assembly department foreman, then senior draughtsman, and finally, assistant engineer.

In the spring of 1923 Laird left the company and moved to Chicago. Some of his former employees bought the holding and on 22 January 1924 the Swallow Airplane Company was formed. Stearman became chief engineer. He designed a three-place, open-cockpit 'New Swallow', the first commercial aircraft to have a liquid-cooled 90hp Curtiss OX-5 engine that was completely enclosed and streamlined. It was the cleanest and most efficient airplane of its class and proved to be highly successful. About this time Walter Beech, who had joined Laird in 1921 as a part-time demonstration pilot, flew the New Swallow to many new records and formed a close association with Stearman in the Swallow concern.

Towards the end of 1924 Beech became involved in a dispute with Moellendick concerning the old-fashioned wood and wire construction still being used, being strongly in favour of a welded steel tubing instead. Finally Beech, Stearman and Bill Snook, a senior manager at Laird, decided to build their own airplane, which Stearman had been working on. In December 1924 Clyde Cessna, a previous Swallow customer, agreed to back Stearman. They formed a partnership in business in Wichita called the Travel Air Manufacturing Company. Lloyd Stearman was made chief engineer, Snook became factory manager, Beech was secretary and Cessna, who had invested $5,000 and loaned the company another $25,000, was vice-president. Walter Innes, a financial backer in the venture, was president and treasurer.

At Travel Air Stearman developed the biplane that became well known over the years as the Travel Air Series 2000/3000/4000, built between 1925 and 1929 and using engines from 90 to 300hp. The first design was the three-place Travel Air OX-5 Model 2000, which flew for the first time on 13 March 1925. It was one of the most successful airplanes built in that period; some nineteen units were produced in 1925, and forty-three were built in 1926. During 1926, Travel Air won the Second Annual Ford Reliability Tour, with Walter Beech at the controls, and Travel Air dealer Fred D. Hoyt, from Eureka, California, won the 'On-To-Sesqui' race, a National Air Race event, when he flew 2,558 miles from Eureka to Philadelphia in a record-breaking thirty-one hours.

The C-1 was a three-place biplane design with oleo landing gear, typical of the period, and originally powered with a 90hp OX-5 engine. The OX-5 was soon replaced with a 240hp war surplus French Salmson water-cooled radial engine, and in turn a 230hp Salmson converted to air-cooling by Menasco Motors of Los Angeles. Price for the OX design was $2,750 and for the 200hp Wright J-4 Whirlwind engine, $7,850, or $2,150 without engine.

Lloyd Stearman pictured with Charles A. Lindbergh in 1933.
Lindbergh's historic solo transatlantic flight to Paris on 20/21 May
1927 helped put the airplane industry back in business and created
the 'Lindbergh Boom'. When Stearman developed larger planes for
mail carrying Lindbergh used one of these, a C-3B, when he
surveyed the Transcontinental & Western air route. Creighton
Merrell, writing in the *Southwestern Aviation* Magazine,
March/April 1936, reported: 'Over a million dollars' worth of
airplanes were sold during 1928 alone, a remarkable record for a
new company and a demonstration of the ability to produce quantities of airplanes of uniformly high quality.'

Hoyt persuaded Stearman to leave Travel Air and move to Venice, California, where in May 1927 he formed Stearman Aircraft Inc. from the personnel and facilities of Lyle-Hoyt Aircraft Company, a flying service that was the Travel Air distributor for southern California. George Lyle and Fred Hoyt were associates in the new venture. Pint-sized David P. 'Deed' Levy joined as a test pilot. Lloyd Stearman designed and built the C-1 with help from fellow designer and friend, Mac Short. The C-1 was a three-seat biplane design with oleo landing gear, typical of the period, and originally powered with a 90hp OX-5 engine. The OX-5 was soon replaced with a 240hp war surplus French Salmson water-cooled radial engine, and in turn a 230hp Salmson converted to air-cooling by Menasco Motors of Los Angeles. Price for the OX design was $2,750 and for the 200hp Wright J-4 Whirlwind engine, $7,850, or $2,150 without engine. An improved version of the C-1, the C-2, soon followed. It had a revised nose, belly radiator, removable controls in the front cockpit for training purposes, and the aileron push rods between the wings were deleted. Used commerically around Los Angeles, the C-2 was flown by Fred Hoyt in a number of early movie thrillers, including *Wings*, the Oscar-winning movie of 1927.

The C-2 was the first of its class to incorporate the rubber hydraulic shock absorber in the landing-gear. A total vertical travel of eight inches was secured through the use of a hydraulic cylinder and the inclusion of rubber shock absorber chord in tension. The C-2 also had a revised nose, belly radiator and deletion of aileron push rods between the wings, and removable controls in the front cockpit for training purposes. To keep down engine cost Stearman explored all possible engines, from 90hp to 250hp, without altering the structure of the aircraft aft of the fire wall. For example, a C-2 with

200hp Wright J-4 sold for $7,850, while price without engine was a mere $2,150. Those tried were the OX-5, Wright Whirlwind, the Salmson water-cooled radial, Nordwick Duplex-Cam, and the war surplus Wright E engine. This was actually the 180hp French Hispano-Suiza or 'Hisso', built in the USA under licence. The C-2K had a 125hp Ryan-Siemens engine. Stearman's last attempt was the 240hp Salmson converted to air-cooling by Menasco, soon dropped in favour of the Wright J-4 and J-5. It is thought that all C-2 models were upgraded to C-3B models.

NC-5415 121, the last of about twenty-one aircraft with the Wright J-4 engine (later replaced with the J-5), and built as a C-2B, was shipped to Alaska late in 1928, the property of the Arctic Prospecting and Development Co. The pilot in the centre is famed Alaska bush pilot, Joe Crosson. After only one flight it crashed on the ice at Walker Lake about eighty miles north-west of Bettles in the Brooks Range. When Noel Wien, the dean of Alaska bush pilots, heard about the crash, he purchased the Stearman sight unseen. He had it repaired near the crash site and flown to Fairbanks, where he added it to the fleet of Wien Alaska Airlines where it carried mail, furs, and mining supplies. Late in 1929 Carl Ben Eielson purchased NC5415 for Alaskan Airways Inc. C-2B NC-5415 took part in the legendary trips to the three-masted sailing ship *Nanuk* that became ice-bound near North Cape, Siberia on 4 October 1929, 500 miles north-west of Nome, Alaska. Harold Gilliam, then a low-time Alaskan Airways pilot, flew NC-5415 on round trips to the *Nanuk* to bring in a valuable cargo of furs. It was on this same expedition that famed pilot Carl Ben Eielson, who had founded Alaskan Airways, met his fate flying a Hamilton Metalplane, in November 1929. NC5415 was among the scores of aircraft that participated in the search for Eielson. Gillam and Joe Crosson, the latter in a Waco 10 biplane, located the wreckage of Eielson's wrecked Hamilton on 27 January 1930. Eielson had crashed ninety miles from the ice-locked *Nanuk* after he had flown a load of furs and passengers from the trapped ship. Joe Crosson was the pilot of the open-cockpit Stearman on a flight to Point Barrow seven months later to deliver antitoxin to combat an outbreak of diphtheria.

Despite the success of the C-2, financial difficulties beset the new company and Lloyd Stearman was soon in debt. Walter P. Innes Jr and some of Lloyd's other friends in Wichita put up $60,000 to lure him back to Wichita. In 1927 Stearman Aircraft Corporation was established in a spacious building leased from the Bridgeport Machine Company where tools and equipment had been set up north of Wichita. Lloyd Stearman was president of the new company and Mac Short was vice-president. Big business methods were sorely needed to handle volume sales and in the spring of 1928 J.E. Schaefer joined the company as sales manager. Creighton Merrell, writing in the *Southwestern Aviation* Magazine, March–April 1936, reported: 'Over a million dollars' worth of airplanes were sold during 1928 alone, a remarkable record for a new company and a demonstration of the ability to produce quantities of airplanes of uniformly high quality.' In a December 1928 invitation to inspect Stearman workmanship at the International Aeronautical Exposition, Lloyd Stearman wrote: 'To weld a future to the present so strongly and so firmly that Stearman products may have lasting character is the aim of every Stearman workman in the building of all Stearman aircraft. The ultimate success of any product is measured by the degree of public acceptance it enjoys – particularly among those who know. Stearman products bear the endowment of the country's best pilots.'

In addition to the light three-seat aircraft powered with the Wright engines, production continued on various models that were all basically modifications and improvements of the original C-1 design. Larger, C-3 aircraft were developed for mail carrying, having front cockpits replaced by mail bins. The first airplane sold at Wichita was a C-3MB mailplane, delivered to Varney Air Lines on 8 December 1927. Varney, a wealthy sportsman who had bought the third plane built in Venice, also a mailplane, was to be a good customer for Stearman Aircraft. (The three-place C-3 could be used for mail or passenger service.) Some fourteen C-3MBs (the first ones originally C-2 models) and 122 C-3B Sport Commercials were built between 1927 and 1929. They were powered by a 200hp Wright J-5, cruised at 105 mph, climbed at 1,000ft a minute and had a top speed of 126 mph. Price at the factory was $8,500. The C-3 gained worldwide recognition in 1932 when Ross Hadley, Los Angeles sportsman, made a tour of the globe in a C-3B. Two C-3A models with the 90hp OX-5 engine were built in 1928, as was one C-3B (C-3L), with a 130hp Comet 7 engine. In 1927–28 two C-3Ds were built using the Wright E engine (180hp French Hispano-Suiza or 'Hisso', built under licence) and a single C-3H was built. Three C-3K models powered by a 125hp Siemens-Halske SH-12 engine were built between February and July 1928. The C-3R, powered by a 225hp Wright J-6-7 engine (J-6 with seven cylinders) proved very popular. Known as the 'Business Speedster', some thirty-eight models were produced between August 1929 and October 1931. Beginning in July 1930, ten C-3Rs (six landplanes and four seaplanes) were sold to the Peruvian Air Force. The last C-3R airframe was converted to a single C-3P with a Wright J-5 engine.

Stearmans were ubiquitous in the late 1920s and early thirties, in use with both the US Mail Service and the Forest Patrol; eleven petroleum companies were equipping their newly organised aviation departments with them, and seventeen airlines used them in the USA, Canada, Alaska and Mexico. At one time the Aeronautics Branch of the Department of Commerce owned ten Stearmans. As ever, one of Stearman's best customers remained Varney Air Lines. During 1929 six mailplanes, developed from the C-3B, designated M-2, were built for Varney, the first five with 525hp Wright Cyclone radials, and the sixth configured as a three-place aircraft with a Cyclone engine. The seventh M-2 built was a two-seat aircraft with a 525hp Pratt & Whitney 'Hornet', for Cliff Durant. The aircraft were equipped with a mail pit designed to carry a 1,000lb payload. Officially called 'Speedmails', they became known shortly after by the now familiar nickname of 'Bull Stearman'. (*CONTACT*, 'a monthly publication devoted to the Stearman Aircraft activities in sales and plant', reported that 'Varney has tacked a name on to their Speedmails which bids fair to stick. Indeed in their district it is very fitting to call them "The Bull of the Woods".') As they rolled off the assembly line Deed Levy took them into the air for their test hops. He flew a Stearman for a perfect score in the Ford Reliability Tour, well demonstrating the reliability of the product.

The hallmark of all Stearman aircraft is that they were well made, but very expensive machines. But for the Depression, sales of the next three models – the LT-1 (Light Transport: three built), the single CAB-1, an even more luxurious four-seat cabin aircraft, and the Model 4C (at first called the C-4A) – would have been greater. Just forty C-4A/4C Speedmails were built, and were basically a scaled-down and improved M-2 (Model 4 Speedmails are sometimes mistakenly referred to as 'Bulls', but in reality the M-2 is the sole model given this name). Prospective buyers had a choice of three airframe/engine combinations: a three-place 4-C/D/E 'Junior

In 1932, NC-5415, piloted by Jerry Jones (left) and Joe Crosson (right), in a Fairchild, made the first glacier landings when they alighted on Muldrow Glacier on Mt McKinley to deplane members of a scientific expedition. By midsummer two of the expedition leaders had died and Jerry Jones and the Stearman were called upon to rescue third member Edward Beckwith, who was dying of mountain pneumonia. At that time of year there was no snow available for a ski take-off in or near Fairbanks but skis would be necessary for the glacier landing. On 4 July it therefore taxied down a runway of grass and mud slicked down with water by volunteer firefighters and Jones returned safely with Beckwith, who later made a full recovery. In 1934 Joe Crosson flew the Stearman on a hunting and fishing trip with passenger Wiley Post, who in 1935 was killed with humorist Will Rogers in a crash in Alaska.

NC-5415 also did duty as a floatplane surveying new routes across Alaska's wild interior. In 1938 the Stearman was sold to Cordova Air Service and on 1 August 1939 it had a forced landing west of Mt Wrangell, after running out of fuel. After thirty years on the banks of the Dadina River near Mt Wrangell NC-5415 was retrieved by Jack E. Wilson, who turned the wreckage over to Alaska Airlines. It was salvaged and shipped to Seattle in 1968. NC-5415 was the subject of a lengthy restoration between 1969 and 1978 by Les and Janet Kares of Stevensville, Montana. Over the Bitterroot Valley in western Montana, on 28 October 1978, Les Kares piloted NC-5415 on its first flight in forty years after taking off from a small field at Stevensville, Montana. In 1992 Les and Janet Kares sold NC-5415 to the Alaska Aviation Heritage Museum at Lake Hood where it is now on permanent display. *(Les Kares)*

Speedmail' sport model (the 4C, for instance, retailed at $12,500), and single-seat 4-CM/DM/EM 'Senior Speedmail' with a mail pit replacing the front cockpit. The 4-CM/DM/EM series was one of only a few aircraft ever designed specifically to carry mail, joining a tiny but illustrious fraternity which included the Pitcairn Mailwing, Boeing 40 and Douglas M-4. All had been designed in the late 1920s to replace the Liberty-powered DH-4 and other ill-suited aircraft for use on civilian air mail routes (CAMs). The Speedmail became the fastest aircraft in the US in the 1930s and was the pride of mainplane fleets.

In 1929 the reputation of Stearman airplanes as well as the growth of this Middle Western company, interested business leaders who were then organising the United Aircraft & Transport Co., controller of several airlines known collectively as United Airlines. They also manufactured Pratt & Whitney engines and Hamilton-Standard propellers, plus Boeing, Hamilton, Sikorsky, and Vought airplanes. The corporation purchased all stock of the Stearman Aircraft Company and on 15 August 1929 it became part of the vast United Aircraft and Transport empire. Lloyd Stearman retained his position as president; Schaefer was appointed vice-president in charge of sales and Mac Short, vice-president and chief engineer. Walter Innes was made business manager. Work began on a new plant adjacent to the original Wichita Municipal airport (now McConnell AFB) south-east of the town.

On 20 October 1929 'Black Tuesday', the Wall Street Crash, brought the aircraft industry to a virtual standstill. Stearman had to build biplanes on specific order only, but by taking in maintenance and component work from other companies it managed to fight its way through the worst days of the Depression and work on the new plant continued. On 10 November 1930 the main building, measuring 200ft by 420ft with 84,000 square feet of floor space capable of housing 60 aircraft, was opened. The adjoining administration building, built in Spanish style and measuring 55ft by 160ft, housed the engineering department, general and administrative offices and cafeteria.

In December 1930 Lloyd Stearman resigned as president, and in June 1931 he left the company for California to become associated with Robert Gross and Walter T. Varney. The Stearman-Varney Company was established and Stearman began designing a new twin-engined airplane. On 6 June 1932 the bankrupt Lockheed Aircraft Company was bought by Stearman, Gross, Tom Ryan, Varney and one other associate, for $40,000. The judge of the bankruptcy court said, 'I sure hope you fellows know what you're doing.' Gross became chairman of the board and treasurer,

C-3B/-3MB, c/n 207, NC6496, was manufactured on 10 October 1928 under Aircraft Type Certificate #137 at Wichita and purchased by Continental Airlines at Cleveland, Ohio on 22 December 1928. On 14 February 1930 the aircraft was sold to Universal Aviation Corporation of St Louis, Missouri. Early in 1931 it was modified to C-3MB configuration and went on to fly with Interstate Airlines and American Airways, both of Robertson, Missouri. On 1 June 1934 #207 was sold to Greer Flying Service of Huges, Arkansas, who obtained a licence as a C-3B, and soon converted it to a duster. On 6 August 1936 the C-3B, now registered as NR6496, was sold to Brazos Varisco (Texas Dusting Service) of Bryan, Texas. Eighteen days after purchase it sustained major damage in a storm and was rebuilt by North Texas Agricultural College at Arlington, 20 May 1937. On 10 April 1943 it was sold, along with NR6253, NR8814 and NR3863, to Delta Air Corp, of Monroe, Louisiana. On 3 August 1945 Jack Sweetser of Lodi, California bought it. (Sweetser also owned NR6101 at this time.) On 20 March 1946 the Wright engine was replaced with a Continental W-670, a tailwheel was installed and the aircraft was used in southern California agricultural flying until 1956. After storage, on 14 January 1967 it was sold to Charles Herr of Knight's Landing, Ca., and on 19 May 1980 it was licensed for flight testing and granted a Supplemental Type Certificate in 1984 to use the Continental 220hp W670 and steerable tailwheel off a PT-17. It was sold to Dennis Strong of Penryn, Ca. on 26 June 1991 and he sold it to Dennis Blankenbaker of Waller, Texas on 28 July 1993. Today NC6496 looks and flies much the way it did in 1928.
(Anthony P. Banham)

C/n 122, Registration No. 5600, the single C-3H built using a Salmson 240hp engine converted to air cooling by Menasco Motors. *(Via Mike O'Leary)*

while Stearman became vice-president of sales. Lloyd proceeded to design the Lockheed Model 10, which was stretched to become the Model 12 (Amelia Earhart's plane, the first Electra) and again to become the Model 18 (Lodestar). In 1932, at the age of thirty-four, Stearman became president of Lockheed Aircraft Corporation. He held this position for three years before moving on again. The period from 1936 to 1938 was spent as president of the Stearman-Hammond Aircraft Corporation of San Francisco.

8828, c/n 5001, the first of 38 C-3R Business Speedsters, built in August 1929. Stearman Aircraft retained the aircraft and for three years used it as a factory test aircraft. Hanford Airlines bought 8828 from Stearman Aircraft in 1932 and it joined the fleet of the red overall colour scheme of Hanfords, Tri-State Airlines, Sioux City, Iowa. Four years later, in 1936, Hanford sold it to Speed Hanzlik, where it remained until 1970 when it was sold to Perrotti Brothers. It was later purchased by Jack Griener, then Doyle Cotton, Jim Younkin and Joe Corr. Current owner is Ralph Graham of Mendota Heights, MN. *(Eric Lundahl)*

1931 C-3R NC799H, c/n 5037, on final to Harvard, Illinois, in the hands of pilot and owner Tom Lowe. The Wright Whirlwind 240 gave a top speed of 133 mph and a cruise of 110 mph for about 605 miles. Service ceiling was 16,000ft and climb at sea level 1,000ft per minute. The fuselage was constructed of welded steel tubing, fabric covered, and the original wings were Stearman No. 2 airfoil section, laminated spruce spars, mahogany gusseted spruce ribs, fabric covered. The landing-gear comprised Kelsey-Hayes 30x5 wheels and brakes and Stearman rubber-draulic shock absorbers were fitted. Fuel capacity is sixty-six US gallons. *(Bob Jesko)*

C-3R c/n 5037, NC794H was beautifully restored by Garth Carrier for Jeff Robinson and is now owned by Willis Allen of San Diego, California. *(Willis Allen)*

Each C-3R cost $8,500 at the factory. 8822, C/N 5002 was sold to Chicago & Southern Airlines on 20 November 1935. It was sold again on 30 November 1936. *(Via William T. Larkins)*

M-2 1001, 9051; Fleet No. 14, the first of five Speedmails for Varney Air Lines. During 1929 six mailplanes, developed from the C-3B, designated M-2, were built for Varney Air Lines, the first five with 525hp Wright Cyclone radials, and the sixty configured as a three-place airplane with a Cyclone engine. They were equipped with a mail pit designed to carry a 1,000lb payload. Officially called 'Speedmails', they became known shortly after by the now familiar nickname of 'Bull Stearman'. (*Via William T. Larkins*)

In September 1939 war in Europe grabbed the newspaper headlines but in Birch Bay, Washington the local paper carried a few small column inches headed BIRCH BAY MEN IN AERIAL SERVICE. It said: 'Herb Gischer and Chuck Galbraith of Bellingham, who has been doing an aerial taxi service at Birch Bay during the resort season, have formed an aerial passenger and transport company, and will operate out of Fairbanks and Seward, Alaska carrying freight and supplies as well as passengers to interior points.' Gischer (far left) and Galbraith (second from left) had purchased M-2 Speedmail 1005 (NC9055), whose history included a period of mail flights 'over the Andes', and which had a load capacity of three passengers and a thousand pounds of freight. 'Galbraith, who is an experienced pilot, will do the flying, while Herb will attend to the business end of the undertaking. These young men left Graham airport at noon Saturday and took Dick King with them, as their assistant freight handler.'

Powered by a 525hp Wright engine, with a fuel capacity of 135 gallons of gasoline and a cruising speed of 140 mph, 9055 was good for something less than a thousand miles in continuous flight. Gischer and Galbraith planned to follow the usual aerial route, touching at Vancouver, Prince Rupert, Ketchikan and Juneau en route to Fairbanks. However, this 'Yukon Adventure', which began the Saturday after Labour

Day (23 September) 1939, ended in disaster. Nearly two weeks was spent at Grand Rapids. On Monday 2 October they gassed up and went off again, but got only as far as Teslin Lake near Rancheria and the Swift River where, on the shore, it touched, bounced and veered towards the water, then settled on both wheels but went quite rapidly into the lake at about a 65° angle. As the wheels hit the water, the nose dropped into the water and the tail came up over the heads of the three men, leaving them hanging heavily in their seat straps. All three got out safely but the M-2 remained at Teslin Lake and was the subject of folklore, passed down from father to son. (*Via Bob Cameron*)

In June 1929 the first of three LT-1 (Light Transport) models, essentially an M-2 with four-seat cabins instead of front cockpits and powered by a 525hp 'Hornet', appeared. These were delivered to Interstate Air Lines Inc. for their Chicago–Atlanta route in June 1929, and were later taken over by American Airways. LT-1 2002, 8832 was the second of the three built. *(Boeing)*

Lloyd Stearman and Mac Short beside 3001, X8808, the one and only CAB-1 built. It was an even more luxurious four-seat cabin airplane than the LT-1 and the pilot was now in an enclosed cockpit. Shown at the Detroit aviation show in two-tone cream and tan, and cream and red, with a black belt line and black striping, the 'Coach', as it was called, owed much of its furnishings to car manufacturers of the day. Among the innovations it had deep, luxuriously upholstered seats with high back support, a sound insulated cabin with 360-degree vision and excellent overhead vision, and cabin heaters. Powered by a R-9-75 or Wright 300hp J-6-7 Whirlwind, in preliminary tests the exhibition machine developed a maximum speed of 135 mph and a cruising speed of 115 mph. The Coach, however, failed to make an impact in commercial aviation before the Depression all but destroyed the market for large passenger-carrying airplanes. *(William T. Larkins)*

C-4A (4C) NS2, 4001, the first of five delivered between September
1929 and May 1930. The C-4A, basically a scaled down and
improved M-2 later called the 4C, whose front cockpit was replaced
by a mail pit, was powered by a 300hp Wright J6-9. Stearman
declared the Model 4 'the finest airplane I ever built'. *(Boeing)*

C-4D, NC774H, which was delivered to Western Air Express as a 4D, powered by a Wasp Jr. The Model 4D/4DX (six produced, 1930–31) and the single 4-DM/DM-1 (for Western Air Express in March 1930) were powered by the 300hp Pratt & Whitney Wasp Jr (R-985). Both engines had limited TBOs of about 200–300 hours. *(Via William T. Larkins)*

C-4E 4021 CF-AMB, ex-NC784H, one of the three bought by the Standard Oil Company of California in 1930. The original Wasp C was later replaced by a more powerful R-1340 of WWII vintage with overwing exhausts and a two-position variable-pitch propeller and the aircraft was used as a crop duster. In January 1965 N784H was advertised for sale in Idaho. The late John N. Paterson of Fort William, Ontario, a WWII fighter pilot who had generously donated his Spitfire IX to the National Aviation Museum in Ottawa, bought it and N784H was flown to Fort William early in February. K.M. 'Ken' Molson, curator, heard about Carberry Crop Dusters Inc. of Fresno, California, who had several Model 4s and were about to retire them and their stock of spares. (In July 1939 Mel Carberry had stepped in and bought a dozen Speedmails, and for twenty years had operated them for crop dusting in California.) Carberry proved most helpful and Molson was able to obtain from them an original instrument panel complete with instruments, headrest, windshield, fabric-covered tail surfaces and a 450hp Pratt & Whitney Wasp SC engine,

essential for restoring the aircraft to its original condition. NC874 was painted in the colours and markings of CF-AMB, construction number 4016, the first of the four Model 4 EMs owned and operated by Canadian Airways, and flew in December 1969, with John Paterson at the controls. In September 1970 the aircraft was put on display in the National Aviation Museum. It is almost impossible to distinguish it from the original.
(Via Ken Molson)

C-4DM, 4025, NC796H, owned and flown by Ron and Carol Rex of Leeward Ranch, Florida, in formation with Tom and Nancy Lowe's 1931 C-3R NC799H at the 17th National Stearman Fly In at Galesburgh, Illinois. These two models came off the production line only a week apart. The Rexes' aircraft originally came out of the factory as a Model 4D. It was fitted with a 300hp R-985 Pratt & Whitney Wasp Jr but was converted to a 4E by installing a 1929 450hp Pratt & Whitney Wasp SC-1 (R-1340). First owner was twenty-two-year-old Aline Rhonie, a considerably wealthy New York socialite, who had obtained her private pilot's licence about four months earlier. She became a well-known aviatrix of the late 1930s, one of the few women to hold a Transport Pilot Certificate. Aline and Jim Collins, her flight instructor, picked up the Stearman at the factory in Wichita and flew it back to Long Island's Roosevelt Field after a stop in Miami, Florida. Miss Rhonie soloed her first personally owned aircraft and flew it all over the eastern part of the US. Some of the flights included legs of more than four hours and flights at night over Pennsylvania's famous 'Hell stretch'. Many happy hours were spent giving the upper echelon of New York society rides in the biplane and taking part in air races and various contests at the Aviation Country Club on Long Island, where Aline Rhonie kept the Stearman. Aline met and married Peter Brooks, a well-known race pilot and socialite, in 1933, but they divorced just four years later.

In 1936 Oliver M. Wallop, of Sheridan, Wyoming, an English earl, won the weather contract and took NC796H to Billings, Montana for Floyd L. Aker to fly. About May 1936 the 300 Jr 'gave out' and Aker finished the contract for Wallop in his Howard DGA. In 1937 Paul Tarrant got the weather contract and brought the Stearman back to Billings with a Wasp 450 and Aker flew the weather contract for Tarrant most of the time when he was not flying the Howard around the country for Wallop to play polo. NC796H then went to Wyoming Air Service, and undoubtedly had a stint carrying the mail. Wyoming Air Service was a fledgling airline that was later named Inland Air and then merged with Western Airlines. NC796H was destined for the scrapyard in 1940, but was rebuilt instead by the Tennessee Valley Authority into a mosquito control duster and converted to a Wasp C engine. It then went to California as one of four crop dusters owned by Mel Carberry and later surfaced as one of two basket-cases in the hands of Gene Frank, an antiquer in Caldwell, Idaho. It was restored for Frank by Jim Kimball of Zellwood, Florida and the Pratt & Whitney Wasp C engine was overhauled by Mike Connor of Mt Dora, Florida. Arnold Nieman of Ocala constructed a new set of wings using the original fittings. It was decided by the owner at the time to paint it in the colours of Western Air Express and change the number to NC774H, thereby recreating the exact appearance of the original WAE aircraft. Soon after restoration, NC774H was purchased by Leroy Brown. He put about thirty hours on it before selling it to Carol and Ron Rex. *(Bob Jesko)*

The two C-4E Specials – 4022/NC785H, nearest the camera, and 4021/NC784H, end of the line-up – and the two-place 4EX 4040/NC783H (middle) fitted with a 450hp supercharged Wasp, await delivery flights to Standard Oil Co. of California on 10 July 1930. The Specials were fitted out with many extras, such as wheel pants, spinners and additional fairings. The 4e Junior Speedmail (ten built, 1929–30) and 4EM Senior Speedmail (three produced, 1930–31) were originally powered by the 420hp Pratt & Whitney R-1340 Wasp C. Many Wasp Cs were modified in their later life to Wasp SCs, identical externally save for a different supercharger ratio to give an additional 30hp. Most favoured model among the Junior Speedmail set was the R-1340-powered 4-E, while the airlines preferred the more economical Wright J6-powered 4CM. (Via Mike O'Leary)

(left)
C-4E, 4023, N791H, powered by a Pratt & Whitney R-1830-18 engine, at Crop Duster Rex Williams's strip in Arizona on 4 September 1954. When in 1929 the Depression brought the American aircraft industry to a virtual standstill, manufacturers and trained pilots alike had to seek out new markets other than private ownership, and the passenger- and mail-carrying sectors. The March 1929 issue of the Stearman Company's *CONTACT* newsletter reported 'Wings Incorporated of Shreveport, Louisiana, Stearman distributors' were arranging details for 'their first order of four ships to be used in cotton dusting in the southern states'. That same year a Stearman Aircraft Co. brochure called 'Making the Dust Fly' said: 'The boll weevil, long-time enemy of the southern cotton planter, has been fought successfully, but by laborious and painfully slow methods, for years. A calcium arsenate dust, when applied to the plants at the correct time, is destructive to the weevil. The dust must be applied quickly and at the most effective time to produce maximum results. Planters have found the antiquated "man and mule method", dusting six rows at a time at 3 mph, incomparable with the modern airplane method, dusting from twenty to sixty rows at a time at 100 mph.' The Stearman Duster was a conversion of the C4E Model. A hopper was located in the front cockpit providing eighteen cubic feet of space in the bottom of which was an agitator driven by a propeller located in the entering edge of the left lower wing. Precautions were taken to insulate the pilot cockpit and metal parts from the dust, all stations being provided with bulkheads and all control cables with 'socks'. *(Harry Gann)*

During the course of the NC485W restoration, Addison Pemberton became friends with Ben Scott of Reno, Nevada, owner of NC663K, an original 4E Junior Speedmail, who loaned parts and disassembled his aircraft during many visits. Without his help the project may not have been successful. In August 1993, in celebration of the 75th anniversary of the Airmail Service, Pemberton – with his two sons Jay and Ryan, then seven and eleven years old, in NC485W and Scott in NC63K – flew the original transcontinental airmail CAM 18 route from Reno to Elko in Salt Lake City to Rock Springs to Rawlins to Cheyenne to North Platt to Omaha to Iowa City. This 1,500-mile run represented the most treacherous part of CAM 18 in that weather and mountainous terrain presented many hardships for the early airmail pilots in Liberty-powered DH4s squeezing a mere fraction of their 400hp (rated at sea level) from their worn-out engines. *(Eric Lundahl)*

4CM-1 Senior Speedmail 4033 NC485W, one of twelve 4CM-1 Senior Speedmail single-place airplanes built by Stearman between April and October 1931 for American Airways (later American Airlines), the biggest customer for the Senior Speedmail, now owned and flown by Addison Pemberton, previously of El Cajon, California. Pemberton had seen his first Speedmail in 1971 at the tender age of seventeen, when climbing out solo in a Cessna. Les Deline overtook him in his Stearman 4E Senior Speedmail Duster NC487W. He had 25 mph and a 1,000ft per minute on the Cessna. Addison thought, 'Now that is an airplane!' This almost impossible performance by his biplane standards changed his mind-set for life. After college Addison built up a stock 220hp Stearman and flew it for the next ten years before trading it in for a T-6. His lifetime dream of owning a truly historical aircraft became reality in 1992 after a three-year restoration project of a carcass – actually the wings, tail feathers and landing-gear – which he bought from David Tallichet for $6,000 after being alerted by English antique buff and friend Pete Pavey. In the interests of safety it has a more modern

450hp Pratt & Whitney R-985-ANI engine (mated with a ground adjustable Hamilton Standard propeller, 112" in length), rather than a 300hp snap-cap 985-SC version (this would change it from a 4CM-1, which had a Wright 975 producing 300hp, to a 4DM-1 Senior Speedmail, which historically is in line with a company practice in the early thirties). Four of the 4CM-1s were a deluxe version of the 4CM fitted out for night and cold weather flying, at $22,000 apiece. For four years they were used on night mail runs out of cities like Atlanta, Chicago, New York and San Francisco until newer types such as the Boeing 247 and DC-2 sounded the death knell of the mail biplane. 4033 was delivered to American Airways in 1931 and spent the next three years hauling mail over the CAM (Contract Air Mail) 18 and CAM 33 routes. In October of 1934 American converted 4033 to a dual-control instrument trainer and used it in that capacity for several years until it was sold to Mel Carberry. During 1934–36 American Airlines Speedmails were used as instrument trainers for line pilots before being put out to pasture. *(Addison Pemberton)*

Factory-fresh C-4E, 4005, NC663K, one of four bought by American Airlines. Mel Carberry's purchase of a dozen Speedmails in July 1939 included four American Airlines Speedmails, as well as eight more from other mail carriers such as Western Air Express. In 1968 Bob Pinney of Pasadena bought three of the rotting hulks from Carberry (including 4033/NC485W) and restored one, NC663K. Its first owner was William Keith Scott, a Los Angeles businessman, who placed his verbal order on 12 November 1929. Options included a reserve fuel tank, retracting landing lights, dual flare tubes for night-landing flares, radio, wheel pants, and a 'relief tube', making the final delivery price $18,107.50, a lot of money for 1929. It was, however, faster than the military pursuit planes and faster than the mailplanes of the day. It had the range to fly non-stop from Reno to Los Angeles and the brute power to climb out of Reno straight west without circling. It was definitely the 'Cadillac' of the executive aircraft of the 1930s. NC663K took its place in the Scott Motor Co. fleet, joining at various times an older Stearman, a Fokker F10 Tri Motor, and a Ford 'Tin Goose' Tri-Motor. In August 1942 Keith Scott sold the 4E to Carberry Dusters because in those years civilians could not fly in the Coastal Defence Zone. Scott joined Douglas Aircraft as a test pilot and NC663K became a crop duster. It was used in this role from 1951 to 1954 and again from 1959 to 1964. In 1985 Keith Scott, now eighty-one, bought it back from the then owner, Dan Wine, a United Airlines captain in Denver, who had bought it in 1972. Wine drove home a new Cadillac Fleetwood with a cheque in his pocket. NC663K still flies and is now owned by Keith Scott's son, Ben, of Carson City, Nevada. (*Via William T. Larkins*)

2. The Stearman Legacy: YPT-9 and the X Series

April to October 1931 saw the last of the large Stearman mail plane contracts completed when twelve 4CM-1 Senior Speedmails were built for American Airways. It was intended that Hamilton Aircraft be moved from Milwaukee to a location adjacent to Stearman, with Stearman responsible for sales and service, but this move did not come off. Instead, Northrop Aircraft of Burbank, California, one of United's later acquisitions, relocated to Wichita and was merged with Stearman Aircraft Corporation in September 1931.

Sales of aircraft to individuals for sport and business purposes became noticeably scarce during the Depression and although great effort was placed on a lucrative market for mailplanes as in the past, this was supplemented by development, begun in 1930, towards military production. Lloyd Stearman designed a trainer, the YPT-9 (Model 6A), to US Navy specifications, with a Navy N-22 airfoil. The Model 6, known commercially as the 'Cloudboy', was reliable, fast and safe and was powered by the 165hp Wright J6-5 five-cylinder radial engine. Six Model 6s with various engines were built for the civil market during the period 1930–33. However, the Naval Air Factory could build its own training aircraft; this, and the lack of funding, meant no military orders were forthcoming. In August 1930, meanwhile, the first Model 6A had been sent to the Materiels Division at Wright Field followed in September by a second (XPT-912), for evaluation by the Army. The XPT-912 was accepted as a suitable Army trainer but the Consolidated YPT-11 won the 1930–31 Army competition for a primary trainer and the Buffalo, New York company was awarded a production contract. Stearman, and Verville, the other contender, had to content themselves with a service test contract for four aircraft each. By December 1930 Stearman had received acceptance by the Army of a contract for four YPT-9s (Model 6) to the value of $21,000.

Walter Innes assumed the presidency of Stearman Aircraft in March 1932 and J.E. Schaefer became secretary and vice-president/sales. In July 1933 Schaefer succeeded Walter Innes to become president and treasurer of Stearman. He must have been delighted when United Aircraft & Transport Corporation, Stearman Aircraft's corporate parent, set aside $10,000 for the Wichita plant to produce an improved YPT-9 design after they learned that the Army was about to issue a new specification and a new competition for a primary trainer. And the specification called for an open-cockpit biplane design! In May the Model 80 development of the Model 4 had seemed to signal the end of the open-cockpit biplane in American commercial aviation. Built to military specifications, every effort was made to produce a sleek, clean biplane. The Model 80 had streamlined wheels, twenty-four-inch tyres and landing-gear, and was powered by a 420hp Pratt & Whitney Wasp Jr Model T3A engine. The pilot sat in a rear cockpit enclosure. The Model 81 was virtually identical but had the pilot in the front cockpit and a single canopy covering both cockpits. It could easily be equipped as a seaplane using Model 3830 Edo floats. By converting the passenger compartment, twenty-seven cubic feet of cargo space could be gained. Only one of each aircraft was made. Produced as an export mail and armed fighting airplane, the

Model 81 was sold to the Mexican government in August 1933 following an unsuccessful sales tour of South America.

Early in November 1933, chief engineer Mac Short and his small staff, notably Harold Zipp, Stearman Engineering Section Chief, and Jack Clark, began a design revision of Lloyd Stearman's Model 6. Incredibly, they produced a prototype in just sixty days. Zipp and Clark drew inspiration from the Boeing 203 three-seat primary trainer, and design principles from the Stearman C3R and C3E models. At first their new design was called the Model 6-L because of the higher performance 215hp military Lycoming R-680-3 engine used in place of the Wright R-540-E which had powered the Model 6. However, just about all resemblance to the Model 6 disappeared with the incorporation of a full cantilever landing-gear, ailerons on the lower wings only, N-22 airfoil, a modified tail unit, a rounded fuselage fairing, and even high-pressure tyres, so reference to the Model 6 was eventually dropped and the final version was known as the Model 70.

The X-70 (X-571Y) was strictly a military trainer from its very inception. Though docile, it featured a rugged airframe stressed to extremely high load factors: twelve Gs positive and seven to nine negative. In the words of the wise, it was 'built like a truck' but 'flew like an angel'. Test pilot Deed Levy made the first thirty-minute test flight in the X-70 (X-751Y) on 1 January 1934. In April Levy demonstrated the X-70 (as the XPT-943) to the AAC but these were still Depression years and orders were slow to materialise. The Army had no procurement funds and, also, they did not like the N-22 airfoil, so the NACA 2213 wing section was used. The X-70 did find favour, however, with the Navy. A contract for modification of the X-70, which was to be called the Stearman Model 73, and by the Navy NS-1, was forthcoming. The modification contract was to change the powerplant and other minor items, such as a locking tailwheel. Initially, the Navy was able to place an order for forty-one NS-1 (Trainer, Stearman 1) aircraft by using surplus 220hp Wright R-790-8 engines (the Navy version of the J-5 Whirlwind) which the Navy had in stock in large quantities even though production had ceased in 1929. In 1935 this order was followed by twenty more, and all were for the training service at Pensacola. Being a trainer, and not a high-speed front-line fighter, a 220hp Stearman will climb out at around 70 mph, cruise at a moderately respectable 95 mph behind a slow ticking 1,900 rpm max, and come in to land at about 70 mph, burning just twelve gallons per hour while doing so.

Meanwhile, an X-75 version fitted with a 225hp Wright R-760E engine was tested by the Army in October 1934. Although it was selected as the service's new primary trainer, no orders were placed in that fiscal year (1934–35) because of 'budgetary problems'. The Army was impressed with a further test of the X-75 (now redesignated X-75L3) fitted with a military Lycoming R-680-3 engine, and in July 1935 (the beginning of fiscal year 1936) the Army placed its first Stearman order, although it was for just twenty-six PT-13s (Model 75s). The first production PT-13 flew for the first time in April 1936. Deliveries took place during June through to December 1936. Three separate orders for ninety-two A75 (PT-13A) aircraft fitted with 220hp Lycoming R-680-7 radials, and improved instrumentation, lights, blind flying hoods and electrical systems, were placed for Army service and these were delivered between April 1937 and June 1938.

On 1 April 1938 the Boeing Aircraft Company had stepped in and bought everything at Wichita down to the last rivet to create the Stearman Aircraft Division of the Boeing Aircraft Company. J.E. Schaefer became a Boeing vice-president and general manager of the division. Two years earlier, on 26 September 1934, a government trust-busting suit had separated United Aircraft's airline and manufacturing activities and the Boeing Aircraft Company, renamed from the Boeing Airplane Company, and a separate entity from Boeing Air Transport, had pulled out of United and took

Stearman with it as a wholly-owned subsidiary. From 1938 onwards the Model 70 was built by Stearman Aircraft Division of Boeing at Wichita (renamed the Wichita Division in 1941). However, the Boeing name never caught on, and all aircraft built from this time until the end of the war, although 'Boeings' by their paperwork and nameplates, were still loyally called 'Stearmans' by almost everyone involved with them. (In 1941, the US government began the practice of using names instead of actual type designations when referring to military aircraft. This was done to avoid giving away the equipment, performance, etc. of various aircraft, on the theory that specific model information would tip off the enemy as to just exactly what level of development they were facing in any particular aircraft. In the case of the Stearman, this resulted in the little used name of 'Kaydet'.)

Starting in 1939 the Kansas plant began turning out Stearman primary trainers by the hundred. That year the US Navy reassessed its expanded pilot training needs and how best to meet them. No longer would all pilots be seaplane trained; they would require convertible landplane/seaplane primary training aircraft. Destiny decreed that the Stearman would be built in greater numbers than any other biplane in American history.

YPT-9 fuselages being assembled at the Stearman Aircraft factory on 9 February 1931. Stearman was among the first to use techniques such as welded steel tube fuselage construction, which rendered the world of wood and wire obsolete. However, British and some European manufacturers still persisted in building biplane fuselages using wooden longerons and wire crossbracing, which were a throw-back to the days of WWI.
(Via Gordon Plaskett)

YPT-9 (Model 6/6002), pictured on 27 February 1931, which was completed on 18 August 1930 as a 6A with a 220hp Wright YR-540. The split-axle gear was fitted with Aerol shock struts while the large 30x5 wheels were fitted with brakes. A swivel-mounted tail skid was fitted but later models had a tailwheel. The wing was based on solid spruce spars with spruce and plywood wing truss wing ribs. The leading edges of both wings were covered with light dural and the entire unit was covered in fabric. Each wing panel was fitted with a Friese-style aileron and each pair was connected with a streamlined push-pull strut. *(Via Gordon Plaskett)*

At the Stearman factory on 2 November 1931 after modifications are the two YPT-9Bs, 31-459 and 31-460, each of which were fitted with a 220hp Lycoming YR-680 engine, and (right) 31-461, which has just had its Wright replaced with a 210hp YR-720 (C5) Kinner and redesignated YPT-9C. Deliveries of the four YPT-9s to the Army had begun in March 1931, three going to Brooks Field near San Antonia while 31-459 went to Wright Field. This aircraft was later re-engined, first with the new Continental YR-545, and later the 200hp Lycoming YR-680. The other three YPT-9s also underwent changes of engine. Stearman modified the YPT-9s to take a 210hp Kimmer (YPT-9C) and a 215hp Lycoming R-680 (9B). In an attempt to improve performance, two of the aircraft were re-engined with a 300hp Pratt & Whitney R-985-1 and a 300hp Wright R-975-E (6C, produced as a commercial model in 1933), but were considered too 'hot' for primary training and were redesignated basic trainers, YBT-9. Of the four Model 6 aeroplanes used by the AAC, 31-459 (6008) lasted longest, serving until October 1941 when it was loaned to the Department of the Interior in Albuquerque. The transfer was made permanent in April 1942. Model 6A being assembled at Stearman Aircraft late in July 1930. *(Via Gordon Plaskett)*

YPT-9B fitted with a Lycoming R-680, pictured at Randolph Field, Texas on 15 January 1932. YPT-9 31-459 and 31-460 were both converted to YPT-9B configuration with the installation of the Lycoming R-680 engine. *(Via Mike O'Leary)*

(left)
6002 was completed on 18 August 1930 as a 6A with a 220hp Wright YR-540, pictured with its 165hp Wright J-6-5 Whirlwind engine on 13 September 1930, three days before being designated XPT-912. 6002 was one of two Model 6As used by the AAC Materials Division at Wright Field, Dayton, Ohio, for members of the Primary Trainer Board to fly. The aircraft was purchased outright by the Army on 7 October 1931. On 13 September 1934 No. 6002 was sold to George L. Harte of Wichita. Although Stearman's foray into the military market with the Model 6 flopped, the aircraft did become the progenitor of the successful N2S-1 series, forty-one of which were ordered by the Navy in 1934. *(Via Gordon Plaskett)*

Model 6P 6002 NC787H being flown by owner Gordon Plaskett of King City, California, who acquired the aircraft as a basket-case from Donal C. Noonan Jr of Seal Beach, California on 29 December 1986. Gordon spent seven years restoring the aircraft to pristine condition and it is now one of three known Model 6 Stearmans that survive out of the ten built. *(Gordon Plaskett)*

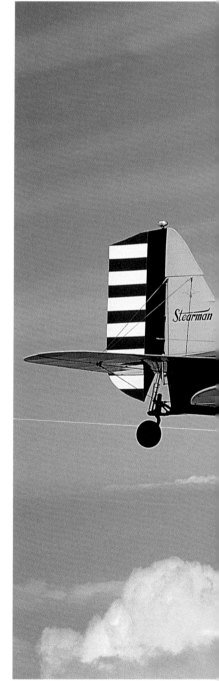

Model 6F, c/n 6003, N788H, fitted with the Continental 165hp A-70 seven-cylinder radial, which received its type certificate on 30 September 1930 and was sold to Skyways Inc. in Cleveland, Ohio on 16 April 1931. While with Skyways it was apparently used for commercial pilot training. At a later date N788H was converted to a 6-L with the Lycoming 215hp R-680 nine-cylinder radial, regarded by pilots as being the best of the Cloudboy series since it produced enough power and was exceptionally smooth in operation. N788H went through several owners and then apparently into storage during WWII. Post-war, there was little use for an aircraft like the Cloudboy and in 1946 NC788H and two others were converted into crop dusters. A Lycoming R-680-B4D engine was installed, the front cockpit had its controls and fixtures removed and a hopper tank was fitted, while the elevators and rudder were covered with 24ST Alclad. In the early 1960s Frank Luft found the now neglected Cloudboy, purchased the aircraft, and began the long job of restoration. Completed in 1966, N788H was finished as an AAC YPT-9 and was an instant hit on the airshow circuit, picking up many awards. The aircraft is currently owned and operated by the American Aeronautical Foundation at Camarillo airport in southern California. *(Mike O'Leary)*

The single Model X-75 (c/n 75000) X14407 was the prototype of the Model 75 series and a revision of the Model NS-1, Navy trainer, to meet Army primary trainer requirements. It was fitted with a 225hp Wright R-760E Whirlwind engine and first flew on 23 September 1934. *(William T. Larkins)*

Thirteen Model 76D1s powered by a 320hp Pratt & Whitney Wasp Jr Model T1B engine were produced in 1936–37. The Model 76/76D-1 were advanced armed trainer versions of the Model 73 for low-budget air forces and therefore designed to be multi-purpose. A Type A3 external bomb rack was added under the fuselage, a .30 calibre machine-gun on each lower wing outside of the propeller arc, and a single gun in the rear cockpit. In June 1936, the first ten

Model 76D1s (76001–76010) were delivered to the Argentine Navy, and three (76011–76013) for the Philippines followed in March 1937. The Model 76 paralleled the A73B1, four of which were delivered to the Cuban government in October 1939. The A73B1 was powered by a 235hp Wright Whirlwind R-760-ET engine, and fitted with .30 calibre guns, two forward and one aft facing. In March 1940 Cuba took delivery of three more. *(Boeing)*

In May 1936 Camp Murphy was ready for operations and by 1937 the Filipino training scheme carried out there by two American instructors, Lt William 'Jerry' Lee and Lt Hugh 'Lefty' Parker, was paying dividends. The two Americans had been ordered to 'teach the Filipinos to fly, but don't kill them'. These were not easy instructions since most of the students were totally ignorant of mechanics and had no experience at all with even the most elementary machines. These men came straight from the fields, most never having driven a car or motorcycle or even owning a bicycle. (This photograph was taken at Camp Murphy on 11 December 1939.) As a member of General MacArthur's staff in the Philippines shortly before WWII, Lt-Col Dwight D. Eisenhower (in white jacket) was taught to fly on the Stearman. His instructor, Capt (later director, PAAAC Flying School) Jesus 'Jess' Villamor, one of only a few Filipinos who pre-war attended Dallas Aviation School and Randolph and Kelly Fields for advanced training, is second from right, front row. *(Thomas J. Fitton)*

Three NS-1s (Trainer, Stearman 1), or Model 73s (improved version of the Model 70), in formation. Nearest aircraft is 9684 and the middle aircraft is 9683. The NS-1 had a modified undercarriage with 30x5 high pressure tyres made by the Naval Aircraft Factory. Originally, Navy Stearmans had a tailwheel that would swivel freely or lock for take-off and landing, while the Army models were stearable with the rudder pedals. Cadets soon discovered that good brakes were needed to aid proper ground handling with the tailwheel configuration, especially with a non-steerable tailwheel. A Stearman does not have or need flaps but cadets learned that their toughest manoeuvre of all was probably in a gusty crosswind landing. All models had only one set of ailerons, on the lower wings. Although it will do all the basic acrobatic manoeuvres, the powerplants were never designed for continuous inverted operation. The 1934 order for the 41 Model 73s was followed, in 1935, by an order for twenty more NS-1s. Both Navy orders were very well received. On 26 November 1934 company test pilot Deed Levy made the initial test flight of #9677, the first production NS-1, at Wichita. The second production NS-1 model, #9678, was flown in May 1935.

The Model 70 (X-571Y), strictly a military trainer from its very inception, was first flown on 1 January 1934. Though docile, it featured a rugged airframe stressed to extremely high load factors: twelve Gs positive and seven to nine negative. In the words of the wise, it was 'built like a truck' but 'flew like an angel'.
(William T. Larkins)

Model 73 trainers being refuelled at a remote strip in the Philippines in 1937. A piece of chamois is being used as a filter for the gasoline. In March 1936 the Philippine government bought three 73Ls fitted with Navy Lycoming R-680-4 engines for a cost of 80,000 pesos, or about $40,000. In addition, the Filipino community in Hawaii raised funds to buy one more aircraft. This Stearman was named *Aloha* in honour of the gesture. The citizens of Cebu donated their own Stearman trainer, which was named *Spirit of Cebu* (No. 11 in the photograph). Altogether, ten Model 73s (three 73LBs with Navy Lycoming R-680-4 engines, in March 1936, four with commercial R-680C-1 engines and three A73L3s with R-680B4Cs) were delivered to the Philippines, the last arriving in July 1938. *(Via Thomas J. Fitton)*

Six Model S-76D1 Stearman seaplanes (76-044/76-049) equipped with Edo 38-34-30 twin floats for the Argentine Ministry of Marine were delivered in August 1937. The Seaplane high-speed performance was approximately 14 mph under that quoted for a comparable landplane model. All models had half-screens for the rear cockpit and optional hard points under the wings. (In 1938 the single X-85 (XOSS-1) US Navy Scout Observation Amphibian biplane was built, but it never entered production.)
(Via Bill Larkins)

PT-13A c/n 75-0027, 37-071, photographed in August 1937, the first PT-13A built. It was powered by a Lycoming R-680-7 215hp engine. Pilots liked and trusted the Stearman. The only bad habit it possessed was its tendency to ground loop, due to the close coupled landing-gear. *(Boeing via Mike O'Leary)*

PT-13A Stearmans lined up as far as the eye can see at the USAAC Training Centre at Randolph Field, San Antonio, Texas on 15 January 1938. The PT-13A differed from the PT-13 principally in having additional instrumentation and being fitted with Lycoming R-680-7 engines. An order for twelve A75L3 versions of the Model 75/PT-13A fitted with the Lycoming R-680B4D engine was received from the Philippine government in 1940. *(Boeing)*

PT-13A Stearman aerobating over at the USAAC Training Centre at Randolph Field, San Antonio, Texas on 15 January 1938. From 1939–41, orders for 225 PT-13Bs with 220hp R-680-11 engines and 318 'D's with R-680-17 radials were ordered for the Army. A further 255 A75s fitted with the R-680-11 engine were delivered between October 1939 and April 1941 as PT-13B and C (instrument trainers). *(Boeing)*

3. The Model 75 Goes to War

In 1938 the Army Air Corps had recognised that it would have monumental problems in developing a tremendously expanded Air Corps. By 1939 General 'Hap' Arnold, its chief of staff, realised that the USA had to plan for the possibility of involvement in the European war and a great responsibility to help its ally, Great Britain. Arnold wanted to increase the number of pilots trained from 500 a year to 4,500 every two years so he proposed the establishment of civilian operated training schools to train Air Corps cadets. The idea was scoffed at and ridiculed in some quarters but was ultimately adopted.

Arnold's plan was that the primary training phase of flight instruction be placed with civilian operated schools where all services and facilities, except the aircraft, were furnished by the operator but with AAC control of the methods and manner of the instruction. In the spring of 1939, Arnold called eight successful civilian pilot training school owner-operators affiliated with the Aeronautical Training Society to Washington DC. All agreed with Arnold's suggestion that they become contractors with the Army to provide primary pilot training for 12,000 pilots per month. Contracts provided that the Air Corps would pay $1,170 for each graduate of primary school, and eighteen dollars per hour of flight time for each eliminated cadet. This was to cover all costs that the contractor had for operating the school. The programme that Arnold recommended was to take up to thirty-six weeks to complete, with twelve weeks each for primary, basic, and advanced pilot training (ultimately these training sessions would be conducted in ten-week periods to save time).

Freshly built N2S-1 Stearmans with Continental R-670-4 engines for the Navy are pictured at the Stearman plant in Wichita on 27 September 1940. They are painted yellow overall (with silver main gear fairings, a feature of all Navy Stearmans until the N2S-5) which earned the nickname 'Yellow Perils'. *(Boeing)*

PT-17s and N2S-1 Stearmans await delivery at the Wichita Division of the Boeing Airplane Company as eight others fly overhead. In 1940, to avoid a shortage of Lycoming R-680 engines, the Army requested the 220hp Continental R-670-4 and 5 as an alternative on future orders. This brought about a change of designation from PT-13 to (A75 N1) PT-17 and it became the most numerous version of the Stearman. In Navy service it was known as the N2S. *(Boeing)*

By July 1939 nine civilian schools were giving primary phase flying training to AAC Aviation Cadets. By August 1940 nine more schools were in operation (by the end of 1940 Arnold's ambitious expansion programme would be training more than 30,000 pilots a year). One such was Darr Aero Tech, about four miles south-west of Albany; 14 September 1940 saw the first class of fifty American cadets flying the fifteen Stearmans available. One of the first to graduate, from Class 41J, was George E. Preddy, who had actually flown 300 hours before enlisting in the AAC. (Preddy went on to score 27½ victories before he was killed on Christmas Day 1944 when his Mustang was hit by friendly anti-aircraft fire over Belgium.)

From 1939 to 1941, orders for 275 PT-13As with 225hp R-680-11 engines were placed by the Army. A further 255 A75s fitted with the R-680-11 engine were delivered between October 1939 and April 1941 as PT-13Bs and Cs (instrument trainers). A further 150 aircraft were added to the PT-13B contract as PT-18s using the 225hp Jacobs R-755-5. The PT-18s and PT-18A instrument trainers were delivered between June 1940 and March 1941. Meanwhile, the Naval Expansion Act of June 1940 meant even more pilots were needed and many hundreds of additional primary trainers had to be found for them. The Navy purchased 250 A75N1s (N2S-1s) with R-670-4 engines. In 1940, to avoid a shortage of Lycoming R-680 engines, the Army requested the 220hp Continental R-670-4 and 5 as an alternative on future orders. This brought about a change of designation from PT-13 (A75) to PT-17 (A75N1) and it became the most numerous version of the Stearman. All told, some 3,769 A75N1s were built, 2,942 for the Army, and 827 for the Navy. The majority of PT-17s built were fitted with the R-670-5 but some used the Navy -4 engine because of inter-service transfers, and vice versa.

Between April and October 1941 125 B75 (N2S-2) models fitted with the Lycoming R-680-8 engine were delivered to the Navy. Some 1,875 Continental R-670-4-engined B75N1s (N2S-3s) followed the N2S-2 models in Navy service, and these were delivered between February 1941 and June 1943. Deliveries to the Navy reached a peak in the summer of 1943 when 200 a month were being delivered. Some 577 N2S-4s, with R-670-4 engines, were built. The E75, of which 1,768 were delivered between June 1943 and February 1945 (873 to the Navy (N2S-5) and 895 (PT-13D) to the Army), was the only attempt at standardising Army and Navy Stearmans. Some eighteen PT-17As were used for instrument training, while three PT-17Bs were used by the Army for mosquito control in Italy.

Boeing model	Quantity	Army Des	Navy Des	Powerplant
75	26	PT-13	NS-1	Lyc R-680-7
A75	92	PT-13A	–	Lyc R-680-7
A75	1407	PT-13B	–	Lyc R-680-11
A75J1	150	PT-18	–	Jacobs R-755
A75N1	2970	PT-17	–	Cont R-670-4
A75N1	250	–	N2S-1	Cont R-670-4
A75N1	125	–	N2S-2	Lyc R-680-8
A75N1	515	–	N2S-4	Cont R-670-4
B75	125	–	N2S-3	Lyc R-680-4
B75N1	1875	–	N2S-3	Cont R-670-4
D75N1	300	PT-27	–	Cont R-670-4
E75N1	873	PT-13D	–	Lyc R-680-17
E75N1	895	–	N2S-5	Lyc R-680-17

8429 Model 75 built

Large numbers of British pilots were turned out at US Navy schools. In May 1941 the Towers Flight Training Scheme, named after the American Admiral who originated it, was proposed and schools were established at Gross Ile, Michigan, Pensacola, and Jacksonville, Florida, and at the Pan American Navigation Training School at Coral Gables, Miami, Florida. The RAF used the Towers Scheme initially to train men for flying boats, although in 1943 some of the output was diverted to Bomber Command. The scheme also trained some Royal Navy aircrew, who after getting their wings commenced further training for operations on escort carriers. The first Towers Draft, comprising forty Fleet Air Arm and sixty-two RAF personnel, all in civilian clothes because of America's neutrality, arrived at the US Naval Air Station, Pensacola on 24 July 1941 to start their flying training. Detailed statistics were never kept, but from 1941 to November 1944 it is estimated that some 4,000 FAA and RAF pilots, navigators, radio operators and air gunners served there. The numbers of pilots trained for the RN was in the region of 400 plus, as well as about 400 navigators and 600 wireless operator/air gunners.

On 8 June 1941 Darr Aero Tech, one of two USAAC-run bases for primary flying training, began receiving RAF cadets for primary flying training in Stearmans. (Five others gave basic and advanced flying training on single- and twin-engined aircraft.) Later classes first received acclimatisation/induction courses for varying durations to introduce them to US Army regulations and discipline before entering five other primary schools. Being 'washed out' was the experience of many. During its existence, 2,000 British cadets passed through Darr, preceded, and followed (in 1943), by several thousand American cadets. When the Arnold Scheme finished in February 1943 with Class 43-D, the thirteen classes had produced some 4,500 RAF pilots from an intake of 7,500 RAF entrants.

In 1941 seven British Flying Training Schools – No. 1 BFTS, Terrell, Texas; No. 2 BFTS War Eagle Field, Polaris Flight Academy, Lancaster, California; No. 3 BFTS

Spartan School of Aeronautics, Miami, Oklahoma (PT-19); No. 4 BFTS Falcon Field, Mesa, Arizona; No. 5 BFTS Clewiston, Florida; and No. 6 BFTS Ponca City, Oklahoma – were established. (No. 7 BFTS Sweetwater, Texas finished after just one primary course.) All were civilian operated and run with civilian American flying and ground instructors, and a small RAF supervisory staff. Aircraft were a mixture of PT-13, -17 and -18 Stearmans, Vultee BT-13As and North American AT-6As loaned by the USAAC. More than 7,000 pilots were produced for the RAF by the BFTSs by the war's end.

At the time of the bombing of Pearl Harbor, 7 December 1941, the number of civilian flying schools reached a peak with no fewer than forty-one in the USA. In the Philippines, the first warning of the Pearl Harbor disaster was received on 8 December between 0300 and 0330 hours local time. On 15 August 1940 the PAAC had been absorbed into the US Armed Forces in the Far East. It was devastating news, made even more depressing by the certain knowledge that the island chain would be next. Total losses in the first two days of the attacks were over ninety aircraft, among them several Stearmans. At noon on 10 December, Captain Jesus Villamor, CO of the 6th Pursuit Squadron, led six of his obsolete ex-USAAC Boeing P-26s to intercept the Japanese bombers. Jess was able to claim one bomber destroyed and several damaged for no loss. By the 13th all surviving aircraft – 12 P-40s, six P-35s and several of the Stearman trainers – were formed into the 24th Pursuit squadrons. These men flew bombing and strafing missions in support of the ground troops as well as supply runs to Bataan and Corregidor. They carried on well into 1942.

On 9 February 1942, Captain Villamor and cameraman M/Sgt Juan Abanes in a Stearman with a pair of .30 machine-guns added to the lower wings, took off from Cabacoben Field, with the last six surviving P-40s as an escort, and courageously photographed Japanese gun emplacements from 1,000ft over the Cavite area. For fifteen minutes, Abanes was able to take a hundred photographs of the suspected locations. Coming back, Jess flew over the fort at Corregidor to try to raise the morale of the troops there by doing some stunting but was attacked by eight Zeros. Villamor went into a steep dive. The Stearman's wings bent as he pulled out of the dive and headed for home but one Zero shot up the Stearman as Jess came into land. Jess and Abanes ran for it with the film. It was sent to Corregidor by PT boat and the photos taken allowed the pinpointing of numerous enemy positions. The heavy gun crews of Corregidor were able to destroy Japanese troop concentrations, artillery emplacements, and supply points. The enemy was forced to withdraw to a safer area away from the beach and out of effective range. The story of the flight was broadcast over the Voice of Freedom network as one of the few victories of the period. Villamor's reward was a rare bottle of Scotch, which he shared with other pilots and crews.

Throughout the spring of 1942, a group of Filipino cadets flew three Stearman trainers on combat missions. The cadets had mounted two machine-guns on each aircraft's top wings, WW1 fashion. They flew re-supply and reconnaissance missions all over Cebu province, until accidents and primitive conditions finished all three aircraft. The pilots and ground crews then joined resistance groups in the hills and did not reappear until 1945. (After the war Villamor was appointed director of the Bureau of Aeronautics for the Philippines. Later, he returned to the USA. Colonel Villamor died just twelve days short of his 57th birthday, on 28 October 1971. As a final honour, the HQ of the Philippine Air Force, Nichols Air Base, was renamed Villamor Air Base on 2 May 1982.)

About fifty per cent of all USAAC, USN and Marine pilots were primary trained on the Stearman. The US Navy trained its young airmen differently from the AAC. Certainly, US Navy training on the Stearman was much more difficult, particularly as all of the US and many of the British and Commonwealth cadets would be expected

Original 1940s colour photos of Stearmans and their pilots are rare. This one is of McGehee Word pictured at Oxnard, California in September 1940. Word 'loved the old Stearman as a student in the Air Corps primary training programme in 1940', and had 'a very high regard for its structural integrity'. He adds: 'It was a little dodgy with the 225 Lycoming we had in our trainers, but it was so stable and forgiving. Flying the plane as a student was a wonderful experience. The wind in the struts and the rigging wires was almost like a violin. One, after a while, could judge the airspeed very closely by the sound of the wind in the rigging, especially throughout the glide and landing operation. The old bird had a rather narrow landing-gear and was a little prone to ground loop if one wasn't rather quick on the rudders. About the only out-of-the-ordinary episode I remember during my Stearman days happened while I was doing some solo acrobatics.' (McGehee Word flew two tours on B-17s and in the 92nd BG, 8th Air Force, from Alconbury and Podington, England, 1942–43). *(McGehee Word)*

to progress later to carrier operations with all its additional problems. US Navy aviation training offered, therefore, the 'finest aviation training in the world', to quote from the NAS Pensacola 1943 edition of *Wing Tips*. It goes on to say: 'From this training, and through his associations with the Naval Service, the successful Aviation Cadet emerges as a designated Naval Aviator with outstanding qualifications for service either in the Navy or in civil life. He is assured that desirable standing and prestige in his profession which is the aim and recompense of the ambitious young American.'

The Navy's youngest aviator, George Herbert Walker Bush, who gained his wings at the age of eighteen, learned to fly at USN R A B Minneapolis, Minnesota, in November/December 1942. Corresponding with writer Bill Marsano fifty-two years later, President Bush wrote: 'The first plane I flew was the Stearman. I was an eighteen-year-old cadet, sent from pre-flight at Chapel Hill to "E Base" at Minneapolis. Wold Chamberlain at Minneapolis was icy cold, but like all new guys I was up for the challenge of the Stearman. The Yellow Peril was safe for aerobatics, but I never really liked the Immelmanns, the loops . . . . . I particularly did not like the "spins", though once familiar with that, you could recover nicely. I froze my face a couple of times. We wore chamois face masks, but frostbite was common . . . If someone said, "Your life depends on it: you must this minute solo in an N2S, SNV, SNJ, F4U or TBF" – all planes that I flew in the Navy – I would instantly choose the Stearman. It would forgive me my trespasses.'

B-75 N2S-2 3520 (75-1297), the first of 125 of these models for the US Navy, with the Lycoming R-680-8 engine, pictured on 5 February 1941. Delivery began two months later, in April. *(Boeing)*

As at 31.12.41 locations of Navy aircraft were:
NS-1   :   42 NAS Penscola
N2S-1 :   86 NAS Penscola
              39 NAS Corpus Christi
             114 NAS Jacksonville
N2S-2 :   124 NAS Corpus Christi
N2S-3 :   94 NAS Jacksonville
             116 NAS Corpus Christi
              1   NAS Penscola

General 'Hap' Arnold called graduates of the WASP flight training 'the best women pilots in the world'. In June 1943 Arnold had ordered the WFTD and WAFS (Women's Auxiliary Ferry Service) to amalgamate under Colonel Jacqueline Cochran, the famous American aviatrix, into the Women's AirForce Service Pilots (WASP). The WASP programme began with PT-19s then switched to PT-17s in 1944. To shorten the nine-month cadet programme to get pilots in the air and in combat, General Arnold copied the ATA female requirements, eliminating the preliminary three months. For over two years WASPs faced the same flying hazards as men. Some thirty-seven WASPs (including eleven at Avenger) gave their lives in aircraft accidents. Only two were on the Stearman. By the conclusion of the WASP programme on 20 December 1944, 25,000 women had applied for training, 1,830 had been accepted and 1,074 had been graduated and assigned to flight duty.

A total of 193,440 pilots graduated from AAF advanced flying training schools between 1 July 1939 and 31 August 1945. The peak was in December 1943, when over 740,000 students were in various stages of individual pilot training. From May 1941 to the end of 1945, 21,302 airmen from thirty-one foreign nations graduated from flying and technical schools in the USA; 12,561 were British, 2,238 were Chinese, 4,113 French, 532 Dutch. In 1944 General Hap Arnold said that the Army Air Force alone could not possibly have trained so many pilots without the civilian primary pilot schools. They had truly done their job well.

B-75/N2S-2, 3644 (75-1421) the last of 125, delivered in October 1941. This aircraft was later registered as N988JH. Standard colour scheme for the N2S-1 – N2S-4 was yellow overall, with blue or red band aft of the cockpit and the same coloured chord bars on the upper and lower wings. From mid-1943, with the introduction of the N2S-5, aircraft were silver overall. Stars were on the port upper and starboard lower wings. *(Boeing)*

PT-17 41-8441 (75-2000) pictured at Monterey, California in 1941 by William T. Larkins. The majority of PT-17s built were fitted with the R-670-5 but some used the Navy -4 because of inter-service transfers, and vice versa. Rudder stripes were discontinued in 1942. Some eighteen PT-17As were used for instrument training, while three PT-17Bs were used by the Army for mosquito control. Some 250 of the Navy's allocation were N2S-1 models, and the remainder N2S-4s, which were almost identical.

A75N1, N2S-1 3145 (75-0922), the first of a batch of seventy-eight of these models for the US Navy. (This aircraft was later registered in Mexico as XB-TII and was being used as late as 1991.) A further 172 N2S-1 models followed and eventually some 600 N2S-1s were built. All told, some 3,769 A75N1s were built, 2,942 for the Army and 827 for the Navy.

Model 76B4 V-12, of which five (76-074–76-078) were built, with 320hp Wright R-760-E2 engines, for Venezuela. They were delivered in November 1941 with a .30 calibre machine-gun on each lower wing outside the propeller arc, and a single .30 mounted in the rear cockpit on a post and track type mount developed by Stearman. Alternatively, a Fairchild Type CG-16 fixed camera machine-gun with sights and hand-grips could be mounted in the wing. Model 76 armed and unarmed trainers proved quite popular with Latin American and Filipino air forces in the 1930s and early 1940s. Thirty 76C3s, powered by 420hp Wright R-975-E3 engines, were delivered to Brazil. Fifteen A76C3s (76-014–76-028) were for use as gunnery trainers with a forward-firing .30 calibre machine-gun in the lower right wing, while fifteen B76C3s (76-029–76-043) were equipped with Fairchild Type K-3B aerial mapping camera installations. (Boeing)

PT-17s at the Jackson, Mississippi Primary School, owned by Parks Air College of Chicago, November 1940/January 1941. A75L3 32496–32499 75-1422-1425, were purchased by Parks. (Earl D. Coton)

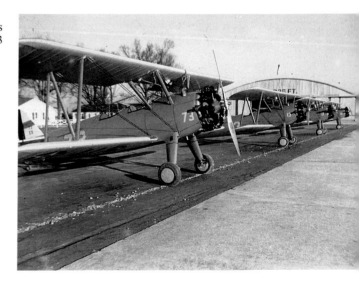

Scotsman William Reid, pictured here (standing) with his instructor at No. 2 BFTS at War Eagle Field, Polaris Flight Academy, Lancaster, California in December 1941, did not see an aircraft until he got to the USA that November for primary flying training. 'I saw Stearmans flying round doing circuits and bumps. My feelings then were that when I could do that I'd really feel I had achieved something. My very first flight was in a Stearman. I flew in them for a total of ninety-one hours, five of which were night flying. We flew without Glide Path Indicators and all the lighting we had were goose-necked flares – flaming oil pots placed at intervals along the edge of the runway, with a double set of pots at the point, beyond which we had to overshoot if we weren't down. When you think of us at twenty and the exercises (loops, spins, Cuban 8s, lazy 8s, Chandelles, slow rolls, snap rolls, Immelmann) we were asked to simulate after instruction by these 'seat of the pants' instructors, you can imagine how thrilling it was for us to be able to do these. This made us appreciate the Stearman even more that it was ideal for these exercises. The one thing they did warn us about was to be careful not to ground loop it. I think this was because at the American training establishments on the Arnold Scheme it was a "washout" offence.'

Commissioned in 1942, Acting Flt Lt Reid RAFVR, not quite twenty-two years old, was posted, on 6 September 1943, to 61 Squadron, equipped with Avro Lancaster Mk III aircraft. He was awarded the Victoria Cross, Britain's highest military award, for his actions on his tenth operation on the night of 3/4 November 1943. Posthumous awards of the Victoria Cross were made to Stearman RAF cadet pilots F/Sgt Arthur Louis Aaron, a cadet in No. 6 Course at No. 1 BFTS at Terrell, Texas, for his act of courage while a pilot of a 218 Squadron Stirling during a night attack on Turin, 12 August 1943; and Cyril Joe Barton, a cadet in 42G at Darr Aero Tech, Georgia in January 1942, for his act of courage while a Halifax pilot in 578 Squadron on the night of 30 March 1944. (*William Reid VC*)

RAF cadet pilots Class SE42E 10 November 1941–5 January 1942 with instructors at the Lodwick School of Aeronautics at Lakeland, Florida. L-R: Jim Shearer, Ron Fennel, Douglas Banfield, George Slater, Jack Frost. Florida, like almost everywhere else in America, had been hit very badly by the Depression. The AAC's decision to site a primary training school at Lakeland, after the winter of 1939–40, was therefore received with great enthusiasm in Polk County. In Highlands County and Arcadia, communities also had reason to thank the AAC for choosing fields at Avon Park (Lodwick Aeronautical Military Academy) and Carlstrom Field (owned and operated by the Embry-Riddle Co. of Miami) respectively. Some forty-seven contract primary schools were closed in 1944. When Avon Park closed in November 1944, some 5,098 cadets had entered the school, and 3,413 graduated. When Lakeland closed on 7 August 1945, 8,825 trainees had entered the school (including 1,327 British), and 6,114 graduated. This school was said to have been the first primary school to open in the Eastern Flying Training Command, and it was nearly the last to close. (*Air Cmdr J.W. Frost*)

D75N1 PT-27, 75-3902 FJ852 (42-15793), one of 300 supplied to Canada for use with three Elementary Flying Training Schools in Alberta and 3 Flying Instructor School at Arnprior, Ontario. RAF personnel had first considered the suitability of the PT-17 for use in Canada in October 1941 but it was not until a few months after the fall of the Philippines, in February 1942, that the first PT-27s were delivered to the Royal Canadian Air Force. However, the PT-27 had a very short career in Canada – just seven months! Winter conditions made operation of the un-modified aircraft impossible. Also, the lack of navigational and instrument lighting prevented any night flying training, which had to be carried out in suitably modified Tiger Moths, which had canopies, heating and lights. *(Boeing)*

Lots of Uncle Sam's Chillun Got Wings

Fighting pilots are made — not born.

And to make enough pilots to fight a global war . . . enough navigators . . . enough bombardiers . . . requires training planes, training planes and *more* training planes.

Since Hitler gave the order to march on Poland, more primary training planes have come from Boeing's Midwestern plant than from any other single American plant.

That's why Boeing men and women get an extra-special thrill when they read of American bombers and fighters hitting the enemy where it hurts. They know the odds are that the men in those planes got their "primary" in a Boeing trainer.

Boeing training planes include the Army's PT-17, the Navy's N2S-2 and N2S-3, and the new bomber-crew-trainer AT-15 in which pilots, bombardiers, navigators, gunners and other crew members are given integrated training. And at training fields in Great Britain and China . . . in Canada, Mexico and Cuba . . . in six South American republics . . . Boeing planes are helping young men to sprout their wings of war.

• • •

The engineering and manufacturing skill expressed in Boeing primary trainers, crewtrainers, Flying Fortresses,* Stratoliners* and Pan American Clippers will some day be directed to peacetime pursuits. Then Boeing wartime research . . . in radio and refrigeration, heating and hydraulics, soundproofing and a score of other engineering fields . . . will make the fruits of victory ripen sooner and sweeter.

DESIGNERS OF THE FLYING FORTRESS • THE STRATOLINER • PAN AMERICAN CLIPPERS   **BOEING**

*THE TERMS ''FLYING FORTRESS'' AND ''STRATOLINER'' ARE REGISTERED BOEING TRADE-MARKS

Fourteen Jacobs-engined PT-18 Stearmans on the line at Terrell, Texas late 1941/early 1942 photographed by L. James Freeman, a British cadet. One hundred and fifty aircraft were added to the PT-13B contract as PT-18 and PT-18A instrument trainers using the 225hp Jacobs R-755-5. The Navy declined the 'Shaky Jake'-engined PT-18 model (all N2S-1, 3 and 4 models were powered with the 220hp Continental engine). The PT-18s and PT-18A instrument trainers were delivered between June 1940 and March 1941.

A PT-18 is refuelled at Terrell, Texas. No. 1 BFTS commenced operations on 9 June 1941 (one day after the first course at Darr Aero Tech at Albany) at Love Field, Dallas before moving, at the end of August, to Terrell, thirty-two miles east of Dallas, when the airfield there was ready for occupation. At a glance, Jacobs and Continental installations were very similar. Both were seven cylinder engines, and used identical engine mounts and fire wall forward panels, unlike the 9-cylinder Lycoming, which had an entirely different appearance. *(L. James Freeman)*

B75N1 N2S-3, 75-7811, 38190, one of a batch of 450, 37988–38437. 75-7811 was subsequently registered N68998 and is currently N555J.

These five Boeing Stearman trainers, fresh from the Wichita factory, fly a beautiful 'stack' over the Kansas plains for the benefit of the camera on 4 April 1942. A75N1 (PT-17) 75-2954/41-25453 is in the characteristic blue and yellow scheme of the AAC; B75N1 (N2S-3) 75-6409 is in all yellow US Navy scheme; third from top this Stearman is in Chinese nationalist markings; D75N1 (PT-27D) 42-15574 FD972 is in Royal Canadian Air Force markings (and post-war was registered N56044); and the top aircraft is an A75N1 (PT-17) for Peru. *(Boeing)*

This photograph of Stearmans under construction at Wichita in 1942 shows D75N1 (PT-27) models being finished for Canada and A75N1 PT-17s for China. The nearest fuselage (centre) is 42-15690 (FJ829). The wings for FJ848 are about to be married to the fuselage of 42-15789 (which post-war was registered N58956). FJ826 (foreground) is 75-3876/42-15687 (which post-war was registered N56862 and later N450HS), and FJ823 is 75-3873/42-15684 which post-war was registered N48792. 42-15981, left, is 75-4144, one of 150 PT-17s for China. For the convenience of the workers, the aircraft appear to be fully rigged before their main gear is attached. *(Boeing Co. Archives)*

Cadet H.C. 'Pete' Henry poses for the camera during primary training 2 May-30 June 1942 on the PT-17 at Hawthorne Field, Orangeburg, South Carolina. Young Henry, who joined the USAAC Aviation Cadets in New York City on 20 January 1942, had never been up in an airplane before. 'My first time in an airplane was 2 May. I was in Class 42J. The first time I got near the PT-17 and prepared to climb aboard, I thought it was the biggest plane I'd ever seen. But I soon learned how to handle it and really enjoyed the short sixty hours I flew in it. The only thing I didn't like was aerobatics and only performed the ones I had to do to satisfy my instructor. That probably explains why I became a B-24 pilot!' Pete received his 'wings' and piloted B-24D Liberators on a tour of missions in the 44th BG, 8th AF, at Shipdham, Norfolk in 1943. (Mr Henry Snr)

A75N1 (PT-17), 75-4140, 42-15977, one of 150 supplied on loan to China, pictured on 13 April 1942. Altogether, 3,769 A75N1s would be built, including 2,942 for the Army. Most used the 220hp Continental R-670-5 engine, although some used the Navy -4 because of inter-service transfers. (*Boeing Co. Archives*)

This B75N1 (N2S-3) was one of the batch of 125 ordered between Feb–May 1942. 75-1180 was its Boeing serial number, and BU 3403, was its Navy serial. It was subsequently registered N5565N, and in 1989, G-BRSK on the UK register. The N2S-3 was the most numerous of all Navy Stearmans. Eventually 1,875 examples, delivered between February 1941 and June 1943 were purchased. Owned by Chris Lawrence, 75-1180 is seen here in the famous 'Yellow Peril' scheme in the hands of pilot Jim Avis over Norfolk, England in November 1992. *(Martin Bowman)*

D75N1 (PT-27/FK108) 75-4058/42-15869 with R-670-5 engine, seen here on test over Kansas on 21 October 1942, was the only one of a contract for 300 PT-27s for Canada fitted with a canopy and other modifications for Canadian winter conditions. It also has a starboard landing light. (Post-war, this aircraft was registered N60821.) None of the Canadian's requested winterisation modifications was ever carried out, except for FK108 which was never delivered to Canada, and at the end of November 1942 Canada swapped their surviving 287 PT-27s for Cornells. Starting in early December 1942, more than 250 PT-27s were flown back to the USA. *(Boeing)*

Cadet pilot John Ware at No.31 EFTS DeWinton, nr Calgary, Alberta, beside the PT-27 after his first solo in September 1942. Two other schools in Alberta, No.32 EFTS at Boden, and No.36 EFTS at Pearce (30 March–August 1942), and The Flying Instructors' School at Arnprior, Ontario, were also operated in Canada in WW2. *(John Ware)*

Assistant Chief Pilot Gene Gates demonstrates a manoeuvre to a group of cadets at Thunderbird Field. Each instructor usually had five students. Southwest Airways' Thunderbird I and II and Falcon Field, carved out of the desert a few miles north and west of Phoenix in the town of Glendale, Arizona, were among the most successful primary schools in the USA. Flight operations began on 22 March 1941 with fifteen spanking new Stearman PT-17s under extremely difficult conditions. The first class consisted of fifty-nine cadets; later classes would be as large as 150. This compared to over 100 in use during mid-1943. From September 1941 until November 1945 many hundreds of RAF and American cadets received their wings at Falcon. On 22 June 1942 Thunderbird II was opened at Paradise Valley, Arizona for flight training. Thunderbird II would be in operation for two years, three months and twenty-four days. During that time 5,500 students were graduated. The peak month was November 1943 when more than 600 cadets were in training. (John Swope)

PT-13D 42-17560/N2S-5 52941 in flight. In 1942 full interchange-ability with the USN (N2S-5) and USAAC (PT-13D) was achieved. Some 1,786 E75 (PT-13D/N2S-5) models, all with 225hp Lycoming R-680-17s, being delivered from June 1943 to February 1945. The Navy took 1,430 N2S-5s. All models were painted silver but the Navy later painted some of theirs yellow. Most E75s were fitted with Haliburton main gear, which lowered the overall height of this model on the ground by two inches. Most Navy models used wooden Sensenich propellers. The Army preferred ground adjustable, steel, McCauley types. *(Boeing)*

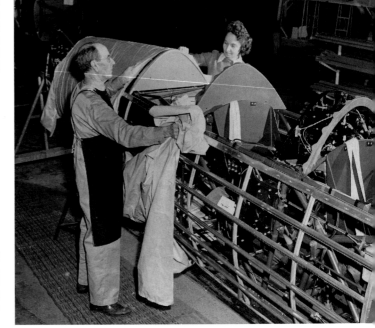

Boeing PT-13D having its fuselage covered some time during 1943–44. The 13D was fitted with intercom, hence the box (right). Cotton fabric was the only type used by Boeing at the time of initial build. More recently, man-made fibres have been introduced which require heat-shrinking process, as opposed to original high taut-ening cellulose dope, to achieve the same effect. *(Boeing)*

This PT-13D, 75-5443/42-17280 61321, which used the Lycoming R-680 engine rather than the Continental R-670, is parked on the ramp at Thunderbird Field after a rain squall. When Thunderbird was beset by torrential rains the combination of rain and fine powdery dust resulted in a 1,000-acre quagmire. The PT airframe and engine were overhauled in company shops during the war years. Both the Lycoming and the 220hp Continental were a good reliable engine and the pilots felt confident with them. It was not unusual for an instructor to plead with the maintenance department not to change an engine even though it was out of time. A new engine always had a few bugs to be worked out, while a well broken-in engine which was still performing smoothly and up to standards was much more preferable. Maximum time between over-hauls was normally 1,000 hours. (*Bob Markow*)

At day's end, students with their instructors march back to barracks past PT-13s on the flight line at Condor Field, Twentynine Palms Air Academy, California during the summer of 1943. Condor was no different from scores of others from Hondo, Texas to Stallings, North Carolina. It had been the first primary glider training school and was later converted to rotary-engined flying, catering for two classes of 250 cadets each. Some ninety plus Stearmans a day were flown and the school had 117 instructors, including a chief pilot, two squadron commanders, eight flight commanders and eight assistant flight commanders, and dispatchers who were non-flying personnel. *(Don Downie)*

Refuelling time and student changeover at a sandy auxiliary flight strip criss-crossed by deep tyre marks, near Twentynine Palms, California. The gravity type fuel tank located in the upper wing had a capacity of 43 US gallons in the PT-13. Oil capacity was 4.7 US gallons, located in a tank just behind the engine. Post-war, PT-13D 75-5064/42-16901 60942 was registered in the Philippines as PI-C543, RP-R543, and RP-C543 (the RP registration was adopted by the Philippines in 1973). It is now registered N4036 and is owned by J. Cowper of Kamului Maui. *(Don Downie)*

Instructor Paul Tuntland watches a solo flight at an auxiliary flight strip in a clear spot in the desert, five miles east of the main base at Twentynine Palms, California. Normally, flights were from nearby dry lakes but after rainstorms the dry lakes were under water and improvised flight strips were cleared out in the desert. Tuntland was killed in 1944 while flying in an experimental troop carrier glider. *(Don Downie)*

E75N1 (N2S-5), 75-8611, 43517, N4325, now G-NZSS, built 10 August 1943, was delivered to the US Naval Air Station at Memphis, Tennessee on 8 October 1943 as 43517. 43517 made its last service flight on 13 May 1946 and was sold as a 'war asset' to John W. Withers of Memphis for $250 plus tax. The aircraft was stowed from 1947 to 1973 when it was acquired by Thomas M. Todd and rebuilt using the original airframe and engine parts. The aircraft is still flying fitted with its original R-680-17 Lycoming engine, installed on 21 December 1945, and McCauley propeller, 41D5926, and is one of only two Stearmans in Europe which still has its original Lycoming engine. During its restoration 75-8611 acquired an AAF colour scheme of blue and yellow. It is being flown here by ex-RAF Red Arrows pilot Roy Booth near Swanton Morley, Norfolk, England on 20 July 1994. (*Martin Bowman*)

Instructor Don Downie, left, kneeling, with 42-1, his first class of USAAF cadets. Downie used A75N1 PT-17 75-1504/41-7945 #13 because nobody else wanted to fly it, and it was in good condition. 'What was it like to take your first five USAAC cadets and teach them to fly? To them you were kind of like a god. If you did it right, you'd turn out the beginnings of a sharp, well-trained military pilot. Do it wrong and somebody got killed. Or perhaps an eager, hard-working kid who wanted to be a fighter pilot worse than anything else would meet the wash-out board and get transferred down to aircrew training – gunner, radio operator, flight engineer – or, even worse, wind up assigned to the ground forces with a rifle or a shovel.' *(Don Downie)*

PT-17 takes off from a sandy auxiliary flight strip near Twentynine Palms. The instructor in the front seat seems to be sitting unnecessarily high. In a rollover his head would smash into the windshield. Minimum qualifications for instructor were 220 hours of flight time and a commercial licence. Some of the instructors barely had their 220 hours; others had as many as 10,000. *(Don Downie)*

Stearman

The King Sisters gather around instructor D.T. Thompson during their visit to Thunderbird Field with Phil Harris and the Kay Kyser band in 1944. Training started at Thunderbird Field with fourteen flight instructors who came from all over, though many were locals. Some had 130 to 150 hours in Cubs when hired to train cadets. At least one was as young as eighteen and Jerry Bacon was old enough to have been a fighter pilot in WWI: he was in the 84th Squadron of the Royal Flying Corps. The average age of instructors, however, was around twenty-nine. *(Southwest Airways)*

(left and right)
Instructor Leonard Pemberton and Chinese cadet prepare for flight
at Thunderbird Field. The Chinese arrived in groups of fifty from
Chunking and Kunming to India via the Burma Road and then by
ship to the USA. Fifteen classes of Chinese trained at Thunderbird.
By the time Thunderbird II closed on 16 October 1944 the great
surge for pilots had finally slowed down. (Falcon Field closed on
11 June 1945 and Thunderbird I closed on 27 June.) Of the sixty-
four Army primary schools throughout the country, only fifteen
were still in operation. *(Southwest Airways)*

Nineteen-year-old Francie Eugenia Meisner was a member of the 18th and last WASP class, 44-W-10, whose sixty-eight members received their wings at Avenger Field, Sweetwater, west Texas on 7 December 1944. 'The Stearman was really like an overgrown Cub and with the same wobble. After my first instructor, Judson Palmer, in mid-February 1944 I was given Herman Fuchs, a tall, lean, raw-boned German whose silence was deafening! He taught more by what he didn't say than anyone. The first time I saw the back of his helmet from the back seat of the Stearman, I immediately obeyed the command printed on his goggles strap: LOOK AROUND. Before solo it was impressed on us how to recover spins in the PT-17 [this one is 75-4626/42-16463, later TG-DOZ-F]. *(Francie Meisner Park)*

Beatrice 'Bee' Haydu (pictured at Avenger Field, 1944), who became the president of the Order of the Fifinella (the Walt Disney gremlin served as a mascot to the WASPs), recalls: 'Those in the WASP programme were prohibited from flying overseas. Two WASPs, Nancy Love and Betty Gillies, got as far as Goose Bay, Labrador in a B-17, but General Arnold found out about it and ordered them to come back. They didn't want us in combat areas. They only wanted us in the States to relieve male pilots for active duty.' WASPs ferried tactical airplanes and flew various types of non-combat missions such as towing aerial gunnery targets, flying as practice targets for searchlight crews, and making administrative hops.' *(Bernice Falk Haydu)*

Silver Stearmans parked for lunch rarin' to go at Rankin Field, Tulare, California. The field was named after 'Tex' Rankin who was killed after the war years in a crash of a Seabee aircraft. Some AAF cadets were fortunate to have the sunny skies and lush green farmlands of central California to provide a wonderful atmosphere for flying a Stearman for nearly four months in primary training. W. Stewart Preston, in Class 45B (in an earlier class at Rankin Field a cadet was trained who later became an 'ace', known as Major

Richard Bong), is one who fell in love with the Stearman, 'especially during solo flights when I found out that I could not tear the wings off no matter how hard I tried. Nothing builds confidence greater than this. Of all the time I spent in training, I mostly enjoyed time spent in aerobatics. The Stearman handled so responsively and was a true joy to fly. Since the need for pilots was slowing down, we were given extra time to train until ninety hours were accumulated.' *(Via Stewart Preston)*

In February 1945 the last Stearman came off the production line at Boeing-Wichita. All told, some 8,585 Model 70-76 Stearmans were built between 1933 and 1945, although when equivalent spares are added, the grand total is 10,346. Included in this figure are twenty-two reworked N2S-4 Stearmans produced for the Government of China in 1947 from surplus stock. At the insistence of the Chinese the first two aircraft were fitted with 185hp Lycoming 0-435-11 flat-

six engines. Boeing considered these unsuitable, however, and the Chinese agreed to the remaining twenty aircraft being fitted with the 220hp Continental R-680-4 engine as A75N1s and B75N1s. Reworked Stearmans were later given to Mutual Assistance Pact nations under 1949 and 1951 Air Force serial numbers. *(Via Mike O'Leary)*

Late in 1945 Jack Brennan, a US Navy PV-1 Ventura pilot and later a Japanese PoW, returned to the USA and was assigned to NAS Memphis to act as flight leader of a flight of three Stearmans to be flown to Louisiana for disposition. About two hours into the first leg, inclement weather and reduced visibility meant a forced landing at an abandoned airstrip. Upon turning base to final, he encountered a mid-air with a flight of three Stearmans being ferried by a group of Marine pilots. The two aircraft collided approximately 20ft above the ground, tumbled and landed. None of the pilots was injured. The remaining two Stearmans from each flight landed and photographs were taken. The weather improved and the remaining four aircraft proceeded to NAS New Orleans. Three years later, when Brennan was assigned to NAS North Island, he was involved in an auto accident on the base and the other car was driven by the same Marine pilot with whom he had had the mid-air collision in the Stearman three years earlier! *(Fred Miller Collection via Addison Pemberton)*

In the winter of 1945 Barney Pollard, a wartime instructor, 'gladly went to Goodfellow Field, San Angelo, Texas to fly open-cockpit Stearmans'. His students turned out to be American ex-PoWs, bombadiers and navigators, whom Uncle Sam rewarded for their years of captivity with a chance to become a pilot, and Chinese who had had prior training in mainland China. The instructors never figured out what they had been taught and because of the language barrier, all training was by hand signal. As can be seen in this January 1946 photograph, where a Chinese cadet 'took off great but, once airborne "freaked out", hauled the stick back and did the easy part of an Immelmann', the Chinese cadets had several accidents. The second photograph shows the results after a Chinese student cartwheeled on landing, proving the old adage, 'Any landing you can walk away from is a good one.' He was unhurt and 'just a little confused about what happened'! Two Chinese actually taxied into each other and simply stated that they could not lose face and yield. One baled out because he said he got in this big cloud and turned all directions and could not get out. *(Barnard Pollard)*

Post-war, Stearmans came on to the market in great numbers and they were snapped up by pilots and used for a variety of jobs. PT-27 (42-15800/RCAF FJ859) c/n 3909, NX56837, later N56233, was flown by Frank Clark for movie work and was photographed by William T. Larkins at Oakland, California on 15 August 1947. Stearmans, of course, have been used in Hollywood movies since the days of Paul Mantz.

This beautiful air-to-air of A75N1 (PT-17) 41-8256, c/n 75-1815/N62770, was taken by William T. Larkins over Oakland, California on 21 December 1947. After wartime service, Stearmans were sold for as little as $200 to become cheap aircraft for flying clubs throughout the United States. This one appears to have missed the indignity of being modified for dusting.

4. Reflections of a Duster Pilot

After the war, agricultural aviation really took off. New chemicals, like DDT, helped farmers obtain bigger yields and aircraft were the most practical method of applying the pesticide. Any pilot with an old plane and a good sales pitch became a crop duster. The industry was young, and it needed reliable aircraft and men. At Los Branos, California, Lloyd Stearman and George E. Willett formed the Inland Aviation Company with the intention of designing a new plane specifically for crop dusting. Soon afterwards the government declared thousands of PT an N2S trainers surplus. They became plentiful and could be bought for as little as a hundred dollars so Stearman and Willett set about redesigning the Stearman for dusting. Stearman hired his old company to redesign the engine mountings and in April 1946 he and Willet first hung a 450hp Pratt & Whitney Wasp Jr on Stearman NR66994. Boeing did the engineering. With extra power a Stearman duster stressed for twelve Gs could lift a ton of pesticide, land on a bumpy surface, and climb out of tight places. The front cockpit was replaced with a large hopper for dispensing chemical dusts or sprays. The Stearman 'duster' had arrived!

In the summer of 1951 thirty-year-old Bart Halter, a former F-89 radar-observer, was one of a 'gypsy band of crop duster pilots making a fast buck' with rebuilt WWII training planes. In 1943 Halter had soloed on the Stearman in primary, but was 'washed out' in basic on the T-6 for failing to notice he had been flying for an hour with his wheels down! A contrite junior birdman had his wings literally plucked from his Lieutenant's uniform and he saw service as a P-61 Black Widow radar operator in the Pacific. J.O. Dockery of Stuttgart, Kansas, 'the king of the dusters', gave him a job. Bart takes up the story:

'Cotton we enjoyed the most. We put out in powder form in still air. We did it once every three to four days, routine right through the summer. We did 15lb to an acre. There was short cotton in Texas, a foot high without high yield. Louisiana, where I did most of my dusting, the cotton was tall, sometimes as high as an elephant's eye. In that case you would not be able to dry out the leaves of the cotton stalk and it would die so we had to put out liquid defoliant and knock out leaves for 3–4ft. We set the liquid nozzles at approximately 1lb per acre in about 35ft swathes.

'You actually tried for six inches to a foot and made your pull-outs well before the end of the field because you couldn't dive in as steeply as you could pull up. So you made a gentle descent into the field and a gentle ascent when you came up and then you went into your procedure turn. This was an immediate turn away from the direction that you were flying. You'd pull up and use your muscle and pull that wing over into a 270° which would put you down on the cotton but one more swathe into wind. Then you got to the other end and you'd pull up hard and you'd dive back in. This required muscle because it's the only time you could muscle an airplane. You still had to be careful because every once in a while you'd feel a "burble" but you got very used to that very soon. The procedure turn at the end of a field had to be smooth but it had to be exactly right to set you back down. I'd say about 35ft from where you put the last swathe down until you got to the end of the field. Quite often you'd fly with lines at the end of the field. You'd be accused of flying under the lines, which I've done only on a couple of occasions, and that was by mistake. You make a gentle pull up at both ends and make a very gentle descent and then make a cross pass and you'd have a nice smooth application.

'The cotton spray was difficult to put out evenly so we had flagmen at the ends of the field who would take sixteen steps, hold up the flag on a cane pole. We'd make our procedure turn, come back and they'd drop the flags and run, before we dived over their heads. We always flew cross wind starting with the downwind end, over-laying passes and hoping to get it out as ordered. Powder went out around 7½lb. Once in a while some fool would hold his flag up and we'd remove it from him. We'd charge him time lost while he got another flag. The flagmen got covered with the poison. I'm glad I only dusted for a few years. The poisons were cumulative. I've heard of some dusters dying later with lung problems. I don't think it got anywhere but to my brain.

'What you wanted was to get down on the crops, not slow yourself up, but just where you licked it once in a while and try to stay within a foot of it so you get a fine, even coverage. It has been known to suck an airplane right in if you dug your wheels right into it. Then it would slow you down to a stop and then there you are sitting in the middle of a cotton field with an engine wide open just mauling the cotton. And they'd have to pull you out and louse up half the cotton, which you'd lose money on. Farmers didn't think too kindly to landing in a cotton field with an airplane.

N2S-3, 07330, c/n 75-6934, NR63519, photographed by William T. Larkins at Sacramento, California on 22 May 1947, his earliest photo of a Stearman with a 450hp Wasp R-985 engine (from a BT-13). Owner Red Jensen told Larkins that the engine had been installed on 19 February 1947. (The unique brush spray nozzles, turned by air-driven propellers, was a Jensen design.) It was not unusual for a pilot to lift one of the 450hp dusters out of a cow pasture with 900lb of DDT aboard, and clear a 75ft row of trees with room to spare, little more than 1,000ft from the take-off point. *Aviation Weekly*, 21 July 1947, carried an article about 'High-Power Dusters Operated in Idaho'. Horace Mitchell, chief pilot, reports on the plane which hit a five-wire electric line near Howe, Idaho, cut every wire, and after faltering momentarily, picked up on full throttle and flew out. Beyond some propeller nicks and minor cuts and burns on the fuselage and wings the plane was undamaged and has continued flying without repairs. Other planes of the same type have cropped as much as six feet out of the tops of trees with their propellers, and mowed willow treetops for about fifty yards along a canal bank without serious harm to the planes.

N2S-3, USN 38393, c/n 8014, NR63555, of Charles Metcalf, photographed at Sacramento, California on 21 February 1948 by William T. Larkins. Metcalf claimed that it had only nine hours' flying time when he bought it and that he personally installed the 'second Wasp Stearman on the West Coast' in this plane at Clarksburg, California.

'A day consisted of two hours' dusting in the morning till the wind came up. Then we'd spray in the afternoon. When the wind quit we'd dust until it was too late to dust. Some of us had considerable accidents flying too late. One time when it was getting late, I was sure I had enough gas in the airplane. I fought three guys who thought otherwise. One of them, a great big guy, put his hand around my throat. I was going nowhere until they gassed my plane up. I guess I should have been glad. The plastic gas gauge was so dirty that when they wiped it off the cork was on the bottom. They put in forty-two gallons. A Stearman tank holds forty-three gallons.

'We never wore shirts (if we crashed and caught fire, clothes would burn), just shorts, cowboy boots and helmet and goggles. There was only one way to clean goggles, and that was to climb up 50ft and spit on them. It was the best chemical of all. Then we wiped them on our pants. We covered up our faces with some sort of mask when we encountered infestation of crickets and we didn't want a mouthful. We pulled them out of our ears when we came down. When spraying poison few of us wore a suit and mask because we would get so sweaty we would practically die of heatstroke. A second option was to cover our body with used engine oil. A buddy would plaster it all over our faces. My new bride Suzi would come out with a brush and bucket of engine oil and cover my body. She'd say, "Boy you smell like money." After, she'd come out with a brush and detergent and wash my body off as best she could. I'd take a shower in the hangar. We still got covered though.

'I wound up in Partyville, Wisconsin, dusting for the Green Giant Canning Company which grew green beans. We'd go out every three to four days and do a different field. I was wearing my GI jet helmet painted a beautiful green and yellow with stripes. It was wonderful flying a Stearman with it on because you could never hear the engine nor hardly a backfire. We propped our own airplanes. We didn't have inertia starters and never used proper chocks. You just cracked the throttle a bit and put a couple of bricks under the wheels. When you got it started then you climbed up in it, either over the wing or around the wing. I put my helmet underneath one of the wheels and a brick under the other. I propped the plane with a little too much throttle. It ran over the helmet and crushed it. I jumped on the wing and stopped the airplane.

'One day I found something better – one quart oil cans. Gee, they fitted nice up against the wheels. I propped it and I guess I had the throttle too high – and my head up and locked – because the airplane lunged at me, crushed the cans and started going in circles around the field! Fortunately, one wheel got stuck in a mud hole and just went round in circles with me trying to chase it and not get cut down by it. Finally, I caught it and got into it. Had to use a lot of throttle to get out of that hole.

PT-27, 75-3765/NR57374 (42-15576/RCAF FD974), of Charles Metcalf, photographed flying near Sacramento, California, 21 February 1948 by William T. Larkins.

Stearman applying sulphur dust to citrus orchard in the Lower
River Grande Valley of Texas in 1949. *(Al Cleave)*

Fortunately, I had the stick all the way back so I didn't nose over. With a 300
Lycoming you could hold the stick in your stomach and the tail would come up no
matter how you held the brakes. And with a 450 Pratt & Whitney you just took off.

'Someone gave me a cloth helmet. A cloth helmet will just absolutely jar your ears
off so you always put cotton pads in your ears. On the first take-off I advanced the
throttle. The engine sounded as loud as it did with my jet helmet on. What I didn't
realise was that I only had about half throttle! When I came to the end of the runway
I pulled back on the stick and went up about six feet. I wound up going through a
poplar tree and finished up sitting on the ground in a field on the other side. I applied
full throttle and got it off the ground with a full load, which was lucky for me.

'One day "Doc" got us pilots all together and said there were army worms in the
oats up in Lexington, Kentucky. A dense infestation was attacking the hapless
farmers' crops from Louisiana to the Canadian border. Toxiphene or Parathion one
time would usually effect a kill. Doc wanted us all to go up together. A group of
dusters would travel north from town to town in the middle of the country.
Sometimes we might be formation dusting with five to six airplanes, flying wingtip to
wingtip, with 30ft between the wings. "Those of you who are new," Doc said, "just
follow." It might have been a scene from a WWI movie as the roar of engines broke
the dawn and the little biplanes tugged at their moorings, blue and orange flames
licked from their collector rings, and we the crews in boots and helmets sipped
steaming coffee from tin cups. The happy-go-lucky crew I now was to work with iden-
tified themselves as "Red", "Hap", "Fats", "Jack", "Pap" and "Doc". That season I
was to be "Black Bart". I cannot say now that I really want to identify with them for
they were flying bums who could handle airplanes but almost nothing else. Almost
to a man we were running away from something: alimony payments, wives, pregnant
girlfriends and some from the law. Each with larceny in our hearts. Each with the
daredevil, the Walter Mitty, the Red Baron for a master.

'I doubt time will ever erase that summer of '51. This was my first experience with dusters or dusting and I had not the vaguest idea of what was in store for me, although I had been checked out in the procedures of applying agricultural poisons to the various crops. One of the most dangerous was 24D, which was used on rice fields at Stuttgart, which were planted in the paddys a mile square. Rice was allowed to germinate, then placed in the hopper and dispensed as though it were dust. When the rice begins to grow you spread fertiliser, about 30lb to the acre once a week. Then we destroyed the weeds with 24D, so dangerous it would kill anything broad-leaf. You couldn't fly over a cotton field with a 24D spray plane. Just a few drops would leave long burn trails. Soon as the farmers saw the planes coming they would start to file their lawsuits.

This 1949 photograph by Mabry Anderson of 75-8267/N5531N, a Mississippi Valley Service 300hp Lycoming-powered N2S-5 (Bu No. 43173), shows an original installation of the MVAS Aero Mist-Master spray system. Note internal wing booms and enclosed engine-driven pump. The aeroplane configuration was not changed except for the stainless steel nozzle extension in the wings.

Crop dusting had become such a sought-after profession by 1948 that some 4,385 Stearmans alone were registered as converted to crop dusting and spraying. Many of them were flown by ex-WWII fighter jockeys like Cal Butler, a P-38 pilot in the 479th Fighter Group at Wattisham, England in 1944–45; on D-Day and for about four days after he flew top cover over Omaha Beach. He was shot down by flak on 17 June. Butler returned Stateside and post-war started flying Stearman crop dusters. 'All operators were struggling during the early years. We took any and all jobs offered. In 1953 I finished my season in the wheat and contracted with Central Aircraft Inc to lead twenty-four Stearmans from Yakima, Washington for the 3,200-mile ferry flight to New Brunswick, scene of the 1953 Canadian budworm spray operation. Just a few miles from Nova Scotia we sprayed their forest for spruce budworm control, completing the massive job done for the first time in history. *(Boeing)*

'We used Parathion which is highly dangerous and is no longer available. I wouldn't put out sulphur which some farmers used. If it ever caught fire it would travel right up into the hopper and blow your airplane up. One farmer said he wanted arsenic put on his cotton, I didn't want to as I'd have to wear a suit. I'd have to land somewhere else and he'd have to bring a water truck, rinse out my hopper, and shower me. He said he'd do it. I asked if there were any cattle around the field. Arsenic would kill them. He said there were eight or ten cows and a couple of horses but he'd make sure they were upwind. He'd put out arsenic with a tractor before and seemed to think it was all OK but with an airplane it spreads about 50ft. The wingtip vortices from the top of the wing pull the air from under the wing and make a big burble at the ends that'll go anywhere. The vortices helped me position where to start in again. Sometimes we'd lose lift. A lot of pilots removed part of the wingtip and put a flat piece of six-foot-long plywood on the wingtips.

'I didn't like the sound of it even though it paid twice as much as normal dusting, which meant three cents an acre for a fifty-acre plot. It still wasn't much, although we did seem to wind up with $100 a day. I said, "OK. Put it in writing, sign it and witness it. If anything happens to your cattle it's your responsibility, not mine." "Yeah, sure, sure." He called and said he had taken care of everything. I put out the arsenic and the wind changed. A little later all his animals died. I produced the letter. I never dusted with arsenic again.

'We made money like bandits, because we were. We did our own charging. There was no elapsed time meter in the engine. No one knew how much we flew, or how much money we collected. Some dusters were prone not to report the whole thing. The pilot got a third of the gross that the crop duster company got. Dust was put out at five cents a pound. Normally, a pilot got 1½ cents a pound, 15lb an acre. When we put out fertiliser we got less. Some of the dusters would put about $25 in their pocket for every $100 they collected and they certainly would not turn in any tips ($20 if you did a good job). No one knew how much money was taken and in all cases tips were not shared with the company. Living accommodation and food had to come out of the third. Quite often we'd take a bed roll and sleep on the ground under the wing of the planes. We'd take a shower whenever we could. We wanted to eat good, sleep in a room once in a while and raise hell. There were a lot of women who loved to hang around dusters.

'Some pilots just carried every nickel they got in a sack inside the cockpit. He never banked it. We changed towns twice a day. He was supposed to send the roll of bills back by Western Union. The pilot might take half. You could end up with thousands of dollars. Pilots might pick out a town like, say, Mt Vernon, or Lexington, and they would put their share in a bank and come back for it at the end of the season. After I'd been dusting a little while and was making something like $3,000 every couple of months, I tried to get insurance. I asked for $10,000 cover and was told that dusters were such a bad risk the first premium would be $10,000! We smelled like money but we also smelled like poison.

'Sometimes we would get a little bit greedy. Green Giant Company said, "Why don't you get the load out tomorrow morning first thing?" I said, "Well, I've got it in the airplane so I might as well get it out now." I took off, went down to the field. It was a little bit dark and somehow I missed my depth perception and ran into a small

Dusting was dangerous work in the 1950s as this overturned Attwood Stearman in California in November 1954 shows. Exceptionally rugged fuselage construction enabled pilots routinely to survive crashes but took its toll on the Stearman population. In 1950 FAA figures showed 4,125 Model 75s on the US civil register. By 1952 it had dropped to 3,917. In 1964, when Stearman dusters and sprayers were rendered almost extinct by purpose-built 'Ag Cats', the Stearman population had dropped to 2,312. *(Gordon Plaskett)*

PT-13D 75-5960/N5195N of American Dusting Co. Inc., photographed in the late 1950s by Mabry I. Anderson. This Stearman, which in WWII had the AAC serial number 42-17297, was still flying as late as the early 1990s.

tree and some electrical lines which happened to be wrapped around a farmhouse and a barnyard full of pigs. I ended up killing the pigs when the wire around the prop pulled the transformer off the pole. As I pulled up with full throttle and a little pitch I couldn't see the little town that should have been there. I had blacked out the whole town. I flew back and forth and looked right and left. There was no town. So I just climbed up and gave up dusting that field. Meanwhile, I could hear something hitting my wings. It was the wire wrapped around the prop. Every now and again it came back and grabbed a piece of fabric off the wing. I found my way back to Partyville and landed. The agent for Green Giant said, "We'll pay this, this one time. You're going to have to reckon with the farmer and his pigs." I never went to see him because I wasn't sure where it was. That was my story anyway.

'There are several times when a pilot gets himself into trouble. One time is when he's got thirty hours and thinks he knows it all. And when he's got 300 hours he knows he knows it all. There's another very dangerous time and that's when he's got 3,000 hours. I got a little tired one day and decided to land on a smooth dirt field. What I didn't realise was that it had rained and it was one huge mud pie. When I touched down the airplane flung mud all over the lower wing, tearing up the fabric. We used coat hangers for metal if we were away from home and cut up an old shirt, slap it over a hole and put some lacquer on it (our Stearmans were grey with patches, flying through trees, knocking the carburettor off, etc.). If we damaged the leading edge of a wing it acted like a spoiler and we lost lift so we took good care of the leading edge. If we'd have left on the spoiler the government put on the Stearman for us I think we'd have killed ourselves regularly. We took it off to make a perfectly round leading edge so the Stearman wouldn't stall out quite so easily.

'Inertia got one pilot up in Partyville. He fell out of his airplane. He had climbed into the Stearman and sat on his seat belt because you never pulled negative G; except he did. He had his trim tab set for level flight or maybe a little bit down. When he pulled up he must have let go of the stick because the airplane dived. He just sat there in mid-air for a few minutes before he fell and killed himself. The FAA demanded to see our seat belts and we had to install shoulder harnesses. I called Stuttgart and got some GI harnesses. FAA instructors would also take an ice-pick and press it hard against the metal tubing and take our number down if we didn't replace the formers.

'One time when we had a little rain, me and two of the guys landed in a farmyard where there was some grass. The farmer gave us food and drink. The farmer's kids asked if they could wash my airplane down. One of the things I was told never to do was get the harness on my Lycoming 300 wet, especially never to try and wash it with any kind of solvent because the wire and insulation was so bad it would short out and I'd never get the engine started. But I said, "Yeah." They washed it with detergent. (Mine was the only one that had an electrical harness around the spark plug wires.) Next morning the other two guys cranked up their Stearmans as normal. Mine wouldn't start. I pulled that prop through until my hands bled. I pulled out the plugs, drained them out and then gave up. I told the kid to get a rope. He got one that I swear was fifty yards long! I thought, "S'posing the other two guys tow my airplane up to altitude and get the prop windmiling. We'd just run the rope through each of their landing-gears and I'd put it around one of the struts of my wing, hoping I got the centre of gravity right." Man, I was stupid. We got the rope ties around the airplanes and I had a big slip knot which I could probably never have disconnected, and the airplanes would probably have flown together out in front of me and I would not have got it started anyway. The farmer stopped me and said I'd have to get a mechanic. The kid said, "I'll get you started."

"Go away kid – what do you know about an airplane?" I said.

"Same as my daddy's tractor. What I'll do is get a piece of wire, run it from one of the plugs to the centre of your distributor. [Each of these engines had two separate ignition systems and each one had a distributor.] You shut down one and let me take one of the plug wires off and stick it right in the middle of the distributor direct."

"That's going to blow my carburettor."

"I do it to my daddy's tractor all the time. Once it fires I pull it out and you turn the other mag on."

The other guys said I might as well try it. The kid pulled out the wire, gave it a crank and that sucker started! We shut it off, put it on the other mag and it kept running. Then he put the wire back in the cylinder. The kid was good.

'I took off and flew over to Mt Vernon, Illinois where I spent the night. I tried to crank it up next morning and it wouldn't work. I said, "Get me a wire, I'll get it started." I told them what the kid had done. They wouldn't let me do it until I went out to the tarmac. I put the wire in like the kid did. Gave it a flip. That sucker started – caught fire and blew off the carburettor intake. Fortunately, firemen put out the fire. They hauled my airplane away and another harness was fitted. It was not an insulated one. It wouldn't absorb water. Cost wasn't a problem. We had pockets full of money (we never bothered to bank it). It came out of the take.

'On my last trip out of Winsboro, when I was due to go back to Stuttgart after the end of the season, Ray Classon took my airplane. It flew well and it had a good 300 Lycoming on it with a constant speed prop that was a dream. Ray was an old P-47 pilot. He really was one of the very best. He hit a telephone support line (not a little rural line) on a telephone pole and he just tore the wing off my airplane. He fell into the hopper full of "Black Mammy" defoliant and wound up in the hospital. It was so strong that if it got on your skin it would cause sores. They wired Ray together but he had what looked like black-blue tattoos all over his face where the cuts were. He later had to have them surgically removed. (In New Orleans we met him and had the party to end all parties. That was the way that season ended that year, and the next, and the next.)

Pilot Lou McWilliams (helmet) of the American Dusting Company gets pre-flight instructions at Chickaska, Oklahoma. The wide-spread operations of the company required close co-operation between management and pilots. At times, satellites were located in five different states. *(Mabry I. Anderson)*

American Dusting Co. was an innovator in leasing aircraft, equipment and pilots to other firms. This service enabled many operators to become involved in agricultural aviation. In this 1950s photo by Mabry I. Anderson, PT-13D 75-5379/N5176N is being filled up. This Stearman, which in WWII was serialled 42-17216 in AAC service, and 61257 by the Navy, was still flying as late as the early 1990s.

'I took another Stearman back up to Stuttgart. It was a real mixed-up wreck of an airplane. Ray Classon had said it flew "terrible". He'd been flying it all summer. I asked if it had any instrumentation. Ray had said, "Well, the compass is good if you're flying north." I said, "Great – Stuttgart, Arkansas is just absolutely north of where we are today." We'd got it cranked up and I was sure glad we didn't have to crank it up again because that was a bear to get started. Once I got in the air I dropped my seat down at the bottom, took out a comic book, headed north and figured about an hour I'd be up at Stuttgart, or Pine Bluff or somewhere.

'Well, sitting down inside the airplane you couldn't hardly see outside but I had a watch and a good magazine. I read for about an hour, then I noticed the terrain around me seemed to be mountainous. There ain't no mountains in Arkansas around Stuttgart! I buzzed every place in town to see where I was on a map I didn't have, and which direction to go. Finally, I buzzed a water tower and read FT SMITH. I was due west without enough gas to fly home. I didn't see any airport. The biggest thing I could see to land on was a golf course. This was definitely the worst time because they had a tournament going on. When I landed I bounced over little lakes and puddles, blowing up sand and disrupting everything. Golfers ran all over the place like a Mack Sennett cartoon. They came running over and asked what had happened to my airplane. I said I got lost and needed some gas. They grudgingly gave me some and I took off again. There were some houses and I hardly had enough airspeed to take off. I turned the airplane on one wing and flew vertically between two houses, hitting TV aerials. There was a large crash which I was sure tore something off my airplane. However, I got it straight and level and cranked up. I couldn't figure out what the big noise was. I turned around and looked at the tail. It was there. Wings were there. Gear was there. My luggage hatch had dropped open and all my clothes and everything but my money, which we put in bags tied in the cockpit, fell out.

'We had to get as much visibility as possible so we raised our seats as high as we could and usually put a couple of cushions under us. Our waistband and the seat belt were right at the edge of the coaming and we were looking over the top of the wind-screen. (On landings quite often we'd let the seat down because if we should make a bad bounce or something we'd cut our head off on the windscreen.) Sitting up at that height we couldn't see any of the instruments. We didn't much care. We never used instruments. We flew by the seat of our pants and the sound of the wires. We'd reach down for the throttles. Sometimes we extended them. To set the throttle we left if halfway down, and when you started bouncing, we may have reduced it to climb out or leave it on full till we went into the stratosphere, which to us was about 100ft. Short guys would extend the toe brakes and rudders. The one instrument that is most impor-tant to an airplane, as far as I am concerned, outside of the fuel gauge, is the engine oil pressure. We would not have seen it up high but it was so important that we'd have it mounted outside the cockpit in front of us. (Some of the Stearmans would really drink oil and we'd use a lot during the day.) By the time we were through we might see a flickering of the oil gauge.

'In the morning and at dusk we'd see what colour the exhaust stack was because it always told you if your engine was running lean or rich. If it was a very rich mixture, you'd have red to yellow flames coming out of the exhaust stack and that was pretty good. If we needed all our power it would be blue or almost white. If you pulled the mixture control back a little bit more the engine would start sounding rough. Also, the engine would overheat and you'd get thumping, or pre-ignition. Or you might lose an engine. I never lost an engine but I always kept it a little bit richer than complete high temperature. We flew at 160° and sometimes I'd go above that and hear the engine thumping or pre-igniting.

'We'd use that colour of the stack and wind the airplane up full throttle and we'd keep coming back on the mixture control until we saw the red flames disappear and

313 and 314/N63585 of Farmers' Crop Dusters, photographed on
9 August 1957 by William T. Larkins.

N2S-5 (43292) 75-8386/N1218N, fitted with a 450hp Pratt &
Whitney Wasp, photographed in front of Sweetser Crop Dusters at
Knights Landing, California in April 1965 by William T. Larkins.

turn into violet and blue and then back into the white. We might pull it back a little
further and when the engine got rough we'd advance it back into the white or white-
blue. Then we would take off. It was the best way to set mixture control for an early
take-off fully loaded. This didn't help the engine any because that was the hottest
point. It wasn't meant to fly that way. It just meant we would burn more oil because
we were burning up the engines. I did not have to replace an engine that year but it
happened every once in a while. Someone would do that on take-off and forget to
enrich it. If you tried to get up to any altitude of course it would get leaner and you
would have to be careful.

'Pulling your mixture "off" with a P&W on take-off causes immediate silence
because the engine quits. What you thought you were doing was pulling back the prop
pitch. And soon as you broke ground, you'd pull it into high pitch so you'd get a surge
ahead. On one particular occasion when I accidentally pulled the mixture control
back, I settled in the next field and wallowed around a while. I advanced the mixture
control immediately and got back in the air. Good luck to me.

'At the end of the season I flew back from Wisconsin with a pilot in the hopper
after his airplane was grounded. The weather was so danged hot, flying low down the
railroad lines we started getting sleepy from fumes. Old Fosdick would see my head
drop and bang the cockpit. I'd go up to 200ft but it was chilly. It kept us awake. Then
the nose would drop. We'd gone to sleep again. We must have gone to sleep fifty
times. When we had a nice long stretch of road I'd land, we'd taxi up to a filling station
and Fearless would get out, put the chocks on the wheels and we'd have a pit stop,
pour cold water over our bodies and we'd climb back. The police car would go racing
down the road to clear the way for us. By the time he was doing sixty we were in the
air.

'A summer of crop dusting ruins your state of mind because as far as you are
concerned you are invulnerable if you haven't got killed. If you get killed then you
don't worry about it. State of mind is not there. You fly everything and everywhere
and people would consider you some kind of nut. The ex-crop duster *really* is some
kind of a nut. You learn a lot about flying from dusting because you know the touch
of an airplane, especially the Stearman, but it spoils you for ever as a good, safe pilot.
You have to learn all over again to fly sanely.'

This modified Medlock sprayer (N2S-4/75-3250, 27975, N7740C) which has the 450hp Pratt & Whitney R-985 Wasp from a BT-113, was photographed by William T. Larkins at Davis, California on 18 August 1964. The normal instrument panel was replaced by the rear of the spray tank and the instruments relocated in the upper wing. The airspeed indicator, altimeter and compass instruments are in the port wing, and manifold pressure gauge, tachometer and tripe gauge with oil temperature, oil pressure and fuel pressure are in the starboard wing. The hopper gauge is located at the foot of the interplane strut. This instrument arrangement was more common in the later years as the Stearmans became more special-ised and improved for that specific use.

Moore PT-13D c/n 75-5876/N1730B with a 600hp R-1340 engine from an AT-6, photographed at Tulare, California, by William T. Larkins on 9 November 1965. This Stearman, which in WWII was serialled 42-17713, was still earning its keep in Modesto, California in the early 1990s for owner K. Leatherbarrow.

William Young operated N2S-5 75-5102 N4756V fitted with a swathmaster, photographed spraying cotton at Wasco, California by William T. Larkins on 9 November 1965. This Stearman, which in WWII was serialled 42-16929 by the AAC and 60980 by the Navy, was still flying in California as late as the early 1990s, when it was owned by J.A. Huey of Yuba City.

Extremely rare float-equipped Stearman owned by General Airspray of St Thomas, Ontario, Canada in 1966 flown by Doug Morgan. *(Mabry I. Anderson)*

Bart Halter pictured in 1953 leaning on the wing of his duster. *(Via Bart Halter)*

PT-13D 75-5556/N4774V (42-17393) seeder of Gandy Flying
Service photographed at Biggs Field, California on 30 April 1966
by William T. Larkins. It has a metallic fuselage.

All red PT-17 N64752/75-2293 (41-8734) of Watts Aviation
photographed by William T. Larkins at Woodland, Ca, in April
1965.

Gordon Plaskett, who began dusting in
1958 and has over 12,000 hours on
Stearmans, prepares to board N2S-5 75-
5617/N1314N after it has been refilled with
chemicals for spraying. Note the corrosion
along the bottom fuselage caused by the
contents of the hopper during spraying. In
WWII this Stearman was serialled 42-17454
by the AAC and 61495 by the Navy. It was
still flying, with Tan Air Industries of North
Granby, Ct, in the early 1990s. *(Gordon
Plaskett)*

N62955 36-11, the tenth PT-13 built and the twelfth Model 75, probably the oldest Stearman 75 flying, or it was when William T. Larkins photographed the 450hp duster at Madera, California late in 1966. All Ag-Stearmans operated with a restricted category airworthiness certificate.

D75N1 (PT-27) 75-3961/N56833 (42-15851/FJ911) at Madera, California with long wings, four ailerons and high tailwheel, photographed by William T. Larkins on 27 January 1981. This American aircraft historian, who has provided many of the photos for this book, has written: 'Before the book *Silent Spring* was published all of the operators had their names in large letters on their planes and they were often at public airports. After that they took their names off and moved the operations to private strips guarded by fences and dogs etc. I'm still interested in agri airplanes but don't bother shooting much except for a different type, because they are all the same now. They have lost their interesting markings and differences. And, of course, it is downright hazardous chasing them on private fields with a camera because they think you are one of those ecologists, "out to document them poisoning the earth".'

101

One of the final Stearman duster modifications was the MA-1 Paymaster, which Air New Zealand engineers under contract to Murrayair of Honolulu, Hawaii began in September 1968. It first flew on 27 July 1969. It had a 600hp cowled Pratt & Whitney R-1340-AN1 Wasp nine-cylinder radial from the T-6, an eighteen-inch increase in the wingtips on the upper plane, a ten-foot-span integral fuel tank and upper wing section, strengthening of the landing-gear, and re-design of the forward fuselage to accommodate the crew. Flying and landing wires were dispensed with. The only unmodified Stearman components were the tail surfaces. The main landing-gear and brakes were those of the T-6. The fuselage was lengthened and strengthened with fibreglass panels replacing the former fabric side panels. The rear cockpit, now fully enclosed, had a bench seat for the pilot and on short duration flights a loader/mechanic. The MA-1 could haul 30cwt on the power of a 600hp Pratt & Whitney. This MA-1, N101MA, was photographed by William T. Larkins at Honolulu, Hawaii on 1 January 1971.

B-75N1 75-6807/N1226V (N2S-3), manufactured in 1942, a highly modified crop duster, was operated by Tierney Aviation Inc. at Bakersfield, California, and was photographed at Delano, California by Nick Williams in the late 1970s. By then farmers had started using natural defences like June bugs against the boll weevil. Insects were ruining well over $3 billion worth of food every year, in spite of insecticides. The Department of Agriculture estimated that if farmers were not allowed to use chemical sprays, crop production would drop 30%, livestock production 25%, and the price of food would rise to the point where one dollar out of every three would have to be spent on food alone. However, environmentalists believed chemical spraying and pesticides should be banned.

5. Rejuvenation and Restoration

In 1964, when Stearman dusters and sprayers were rendered almost extinct by purpose-built 'Ag Cats', the Stearman population had dropped to 2,312. It seemed that the end of the Stearman's twenty-year dusting career would be the epitaph for an old biplane. But the Stearman was destined for a second lease of life. Antique aircraft collectors began buying up the former crop dusters in their hundreds with the intention of restoring them to past glories. It was the beginning of a whole new chapter in the Stearman legend. Surprisingly cheap to purchase, they are easier to maintain than a Tiger Moth. Such has been the enthusiasm, there are literally hundreds of airworthy Stearmans on civil air registers around the world. Scores of dedicated Stearman owners, restorers and potential restorers belong to the Stearman Restorers Association which has members scattered throughout the USA, Europe, South America and the southern hemisphere. All are proud of the Stearman's longevity and its distinguished history.

Fatigue failure is just one of the problems which have to be addressed when converting Stearman dusters and sprayers for the private buyer. Jim Avis of Eastern Stearman, who returned E-75 75-5949 G-BRTK, built on 22 September 1943, to flying condition for an existing Stearman owner, explains:

'G-BRTK is a late-built Stearman but, like most others, its history is reasonably uncertain between then and the time it was sold for surplus by the Army in 1949, when it was supposedly rebuilt. We'd flown the aeroplane in England for three years. At the end of that time the engine had a major problem, so it came out and we decided then that we might as well take the fabric off and have a good look at it. What we saw was really a sort of classic, good stock, two-holer Stearman that's never been cut about, that was just ready to be completely rebuilt properly.

'We took every nut and bolt off it, every panel, all the instruments, side cladding and the controls, bead-blasted the frame and examined it for corrosion, which we were very agreeably surprised about. There's always the chance of finding linseed oil still in the tubes of old Stearmans, but we never take chances and always make sure it is altogether sound before stripping and examining everything else. New bearings are then put in the flying controls and new instruments fitted. Everything is refurbished and as much of the original equipment as we can is used so that although it is effectively new, it's still using as many of the old components as possible.

'The lower wings were a problem, and, as frequently happens with lower wings on Stearmans, especially when they have been used for crop-spraying, there is a real corrosion risk at the root end fittings, together with a certain amount of problems with the spruce in the main spar, so no chances are taken. The woodwork will be completely replaced and as much of the wing hardware as is necessary. The centre section will be stripped, the oil tank removed and pressure tested, all the fuel and oil lines replaced, and it will have a new engine as well, together with an overhauled propeller. Originally, this aircraft had a Lycoming engine. It will be refitted with a Continental.

'The gear is stripped, crack-tested and the main legs re-chromed if need be. The brakes are stripped and new linings fitted – again we usually find the overall condition is good enough for most of the original parts to be used again and that's a very strong feature of the Stearman. It was built so well that it's quite feasible to rebuild any aircraft using a very high proportion of the original parts.

'If they have been used as dusters, as most of them have, then you have to look very carefully at the fuselage frame. Most of them have been cut and re-welded, some have been repaired incredibly badly so that they're not square, and some, particularly where they've been doing a lot of sulphur application work, have heavily corroded back ends, so if you have an old duster Stearman, you've really got to look at it carefully. But an aircraft like this, which is uncut, and is an original frame with almost no damage on it as far as I can see, does not represent a problem in the fuselage department. But the wings are probably the things to look at more than anything because most of them are now fifty years old or more. These are re-done with new wood, new spruce, everything new, including nuts, bolts and washers.'

One of the most involved restorations Jim Avis and his engineers at Eastern Stearman have ever done is PT-17 N8162G. In 1992, Ed Boulter, a WWII Mosquito pilot who had trained on the Model 75 in the Arnold Scheme at Darr Aero Tech in WWII, began restoring N8162G (actually a fuselage, wings and all other parts), a Continental R-670-5-powered PT-17, the 24th built by Boeing in 1940. First commissioned on 17 July 1940, it was given its military serial number, 40-1766, delivered to the USAAC on 22 July 1940, and was first assigned to the Spartan School of Aeronautics, operated by Capt Maxwell W. Balfour, at Tulsa, Oklahoma. The next piece of information astounded Ed Boulter. On 7 October 1940 40-1766 was assigned to Darr Aero Tech at Albany, where he had flown the Stearman!

After leaving for basic training, 40-1766 had been wrecked by British cadet Roy H. Nelson when he struck an airport boundary marker at Darr Aero on 9 August 1941. It was repaired, then damaged again by high winds on 27 January 1942. On 16 August 1942 40-1766 was assigned to Florida Aircraft, Orlando, which was under contract to the AAC to overhaul and repair Army aircraft. On 28 December 1944 40-1766 was assigned to the Southern Airways Civilian Pilot School, operated by Frank W. Hulse, 2156th Base Unit at Decatur, Alabama. At this time 40-1766 had a total of 2,068.9 flying hours. On 2 July 1945 40-1766 was stricken from the USAAF records and turned over to the Reconstruction Finance Corporation, an agency designated by the Surplus Property Board of the US government to dispose of surplus property. It was probably taken to the Municipal airport, Birmingham, Alabama to be sold as surplus. In 1948 it was registered as N52061 at a school in Jacksonville, Florida. In 1955 it was converted to a single-seater, flown to South America and certified as 'Ag and Pest' for crop dusting although it did not have a full airworthiness certificate. 40-1766 ended up in El Salvador where returned to a 'two-holer' configuration again, it was flown back to Georgia by Robert L. McAfee in April 1989 in bad structural condition and with no exhaust shroud. McAfee had to put 40-1766 (now re-registered in the USA as N8162G) down on a road after a severe oil leak threatened to cause the engine to seize shortly after clearing the Mexico–US border.

Twenty years later 40-1766 arrived in England, immediately prior to which it had been flown up from El Salvador to Mississippi before being crated. Although the aircraft was still in duster form, some attempt had been made to return it to standard condition, including the fitting of an R-670 and somewhat token front cockpit items. Jim Avis says, 'It was in desperate need of "the big fix". Accordingly, a "nut and bolt" restoration got under way. Few surprises were found in the fuselage area and, apart from the usual tube replacements, no real problems came to light until we came to pulling the wings apart!

'Now it may be that what we unearthed in the course of removing fabric and separating metal hardware from the wooden spars was not altogether unusual. The wings were almost certainly the originals but it was a new experience for us to find such massive corrosion. The initial inspection of the intact wings gave no indication of what we would find and only when attempting to separate the lower wing attachment plates from the spars did the real extent of the problem become apparent. Two of the aluminium retaining bolts broke in half as soon as pressure was applied to the wrench. These bolts were completely corroded through the breadth of their shanks. The remainder of the bolts were nearly as bad but at least allowed the nuts to be removed without snapping in similar fashion. The attachment plates then had to be prised off the spar, in one case leaving a wafer-thin remnant. All of these parts were so dangerously corroded that it is hard to imagine how the aircraft had made its flight up from El Salvador without the wings detaching in flight.

'It would appear that moisture from the spars had, over the course of years, found its way to the surface of the plates and initiated corrosive action. The condition of the upper wings was not so bad but even these revealed heavy corrosion and a large amount of the hardware had to be replaced. The real worry as a result of this discovery is that the wings *looked* to be in reasonable condition. There just have to be other Stearmans flying around with wings in similar condition to those on N8162G.'

On 12 August 1992 Ed Boulter registered his PT-17 with Eastern Stearman Inc. Trustees of Great Falls, Virginia. Two years later 40-1766 was returned to flying condition in time to participate in the Flying Training Day and Stearman Rally at Old Warden on 3 July 1994.

In an era of heavy metal and awesome jet power the stalwart Stearman biplanes are proving timeless. Future generations will no doubt continue to fly these aircraft on short cross-country hops or further, just as their forefathers did in war and peace.

Hand-crafted from tube, 40-1766, now nearing completion, sits like modern sculpture in the hangar that is its gallery. On 12 August 1992 Ed Boulter registered his PT-17 with Eastern Stearman Inc. Trustees of Great Falls, Virginia. 40-1766 was returned to flying condition in time to participate in the Flying Training Day and Stearman Rally at Old Warden on 3 July 1994. *(Martin Bowman)*

Pictured at La Aurora military and international airport, Guatemala in March 1994 is PT-17 TG-PAT *Tranquility*, which was restored in the mid-1980s by Jorge Perez, an old timer with Stearmans, and fitted with a Continental W670 220hp engine. Owner and pilot, Major Enrique Ibárgüen of the Guatemalan Air Force, has since named the aircraft *Lady Wrestler* after his wife, who is a wrestler. The aircraft also had a new R-985 Pratt & Whitney 450hp engine from Holland Aircraft Engines in Tyler, Texas installed. Some time ago, as in many other countries, there were very many Stearmans in Guatemala, mainly used for cotton spraying. Maintenance for the sixty or more aircraft was done by Marciano Castaneda. Remembered names as good crop duster 'drivers' were Hugo Leppe, Mario Amado, Hector Morataya, Victor Morales and Ed McQueen, among others. During the early 1950s the Guatemalan Air Force also operated Stearmans. (*Enrique Ibárgüen*)

Addison Pemberton in his highly modified 450hp Stearman over San Diego, California.

Tim Beck of Houston, Texas at 5,000ft over Baytown, Texas on 30 September 1978 photographed by Al Seipman in a Stinson L-5 flown by 'Spud' Miller. Beck spent seven years meticulously turning a basket-case into pristine flying condition, using his home and garage as a workshop. The fuselage proved to date from 1943, and the five components of the empennage all originated in different aircraft dating from 1940 to 1943. On 12 March 1978 on runway 13 at Humphrey airport Tim Beck taxied out. The Stearman leapt off the ground, climbed straight ahead and went to 3,000ft! Tim Beck's pleasure was very evident after such a long restoration, which he could never have carried out without the support of his wife Mary and the children, who had to tolerate a 'seemingly unending project,

and in the house at that'. In monetary terms, at $10,670, the Stearman was a bargain. Tim Beck was to fly many hours in 'pieces of eight' until in 1980 Harold Perdue, a well-qualified Stearman pilot in San Antonio, Texas bought 476. He flew the aircraft regularly until 31 July 1992, when a fatigue failure of the crankshaft occurred while he was in the pattern at his home airport. The prop separated from the engine and shortly afterwards the aircraft overtook it, which damaged the left wings badly enough to cause a spiral dive. Perdue died in the crash. His son, Scott, an F-15E pilot, asked Tim Beck to rebuild the aircraft, and although very few components survive, '476' will fly again. (Tim Beck)

Many owners cannot bear to be parted from their Stearmans. In Miami in September 1949 Victor Salas, a Chilean, saw Stearmans performing banner towing and bought 75-1880, a PT-17 built in July 1941. During almost ten years together he and his red and yellow Stearman conducted banner and glider towing and sound advertising in Chile, performed at air shows, and dusted crops for FUMAGRO, to whom he sold the aircraft in 1957. Finally, in 1960, Victor went to live in the USA. Nine years later Victor set out to find his old love. In 1970 he located the old duster completely dismantled in an 'Alas Agricolas' hangar in Uruguay. Then, he decided not to be separated from his Stearman anymore and, would start rebuilding work with the final goal of flying it back to the USA. He did not imagine it would take him 16 long years to obtain the money and the supplies to put his hands on the controls again. When the job was done, both of them had grown old. Victor was 63. He decided to fly the Stearman back to Chile. On 28 April 1986 he started from Puerto Colonia in Uruguay to Santiago, Chile, via Buenos Aires and Beriloche in Argentina. He did not imagine that the desolate Argentine pampas and Andes mountains would be a formidable barrier for him and his Stearman.

The old plane took revenge by giving him quite a number of frights during the flight across the mountains and over the Chilean valley. Ultimately, the aircraft never went to America. In July 1989 Mr Salas died and, as was his wish, CX-AXI Victor was presented to the Chilean National Aviation Museum for public display. (Via Victor Salas Jr.)

Model 75s over Blickling Hall, Norfolk, England on 22 January 1994 photographed by Martin Bowman with Jim Avis at the controls of the camera ship. In WWII Blickling Hall was used as an officers' mess by RAF medium bomber crews from Oulton airfield nearby and the lake was put to use for dinghy drills. The all-silver A75N1 PT-17 N50755 75-4020 with Continental R-670 is flown by Bruce Monk with son Andy in the front seat. '118' in AAC blue and yellow is PT-13A 75-118, the last PT-13A built, which was delivered to Randolph Field, Texas as 38-470. It is now owned by Eric Hopper. 75-118 is being flown here by Gerry Honey, who has over 6,000 hours in over a score of different types of aircraft, including the Gnat and the Harrier. He has also led the Piston Provost formation team. The all-red N3922B is being flown by Dave Bagshaw AFC, a 41 Squadron Jaguar pilot at RAF Coltishall, Norfolk until retirement in February 1992. He flew twenty-three missions, including five bombing operations, in the Gulf War. He has no fewer than 9,660 hours, 4,200 of which are on Jaguars. These three fast-jet pilots make up the Stearman Display Team at Swanton Morley and they perform regularly at air shows and open days each season.

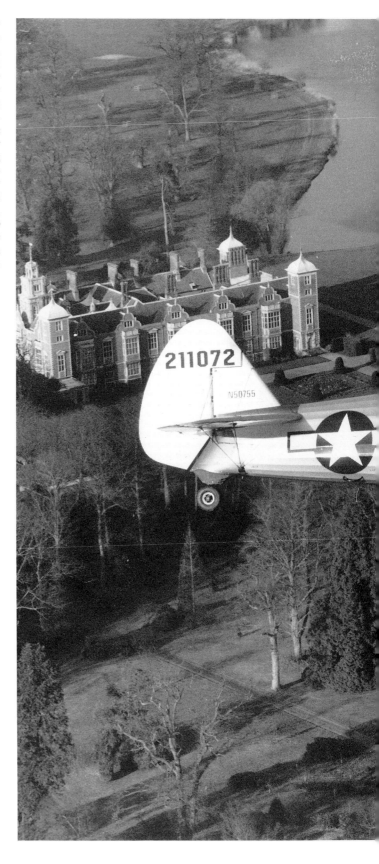

Tom Forys in N65688 over the Chicago lake front photographed by Bob Jesko near the 110-storey, 1,454ft-high Sears Tower, the USA's tallest building. This N2S-5, 75-8469, Bu No. 43375, was rebuilt by Pete Jones of Air Repair in Cleveland, Miss. Unfortunately, the aircraft was destroyed several years later in an accident by its new owner. Jones has now restored over 1,000 Stearmans to as-new condition.

Tom Forys in N2S-3 N57315 over Galesburg, Illinois. Each September Galesburg stages the largest fly-in by Stearmans anywhere in the world. *(Bob Jesko)*

Continental and Lycoming-powered Stearmans. In 1940, to avoid
a shortage of Lycoming R-680 engines, the Army requested the
220hp Continental R-670-4 and 5 as an alternative on future orders.
This brought about a change of designation from PT-13 (A75) to
PT-17 (A75N1) and it became the most numerous version of the
Stearman. *(Martin Bowman)*

A Stearman remains an attractive proposition from any angle, as this photograph of 42-11072 N50755, PT-13A, 75-118, and N3922B (restored by Air Repairs Ltd, of Cleveland, USA), taken by Martin Bowman, shows.

Tom Forys in N2S-3 N55070 on dawn patrol to Monmouth,
Illinois during the Stearman fly-in at Galesburg, beautifully
photographed by Bob Jesko.

Stearman silhouetted in winter sunshine. *(Martin Bowman)*

Stearmans in the snow at Swanton Morley, Norfolk, England, photographed in November 1994 by Martin Bowman. N3922B is a very late-build E75N1 PT-13D, fitted with a Continental W-670-6 engine and is owned and operated by Mr Peter Hoffman, a Suffolk farmer. It is unusual in that it is in 1930s style maroon. Both Stearmans have been restored to pristine condition after rebuilds at Eastern Stearman.

'28' piloted by Dave Bagshaw with Ray 'Bob' White in the front cockpit. In July 1942 White soloed in the Stearman at Darr Aero Tech, Albany, Georgia and he later flew Spitfires in the Mediterranean. Up until 1943, 2,000 British cadets passed through Darr, and were followed by several thousand American cadets. '28' is owned by fellow Darr trainee Ed Boulter, and appropriately, therefore, '28' has the Arnold Scheme motif on the starboard side of the fuselage. *(Martin Bowman)*

(next page)
PT-13D 75-5028 '379' (G-ILLE). *(Martin Bowman)*

450hp E75 PT-13D 75-5093 owned and flown by Peter Stanitzeck which is based in the south of France. *(Martin Bowman)*

300hp-powered '669', and PT-17A G-BAVO '26', flown by Vicky Shaw, skirting the fenlands of north Cambridgeshire, England on a glorious June morning. '26' is actually 42-17496, an A75N1 and ex-Israeli AF 4X-AIH, a rare night-flyable version. *(Martin Bowman)*

'669', a 300hp Lycoming-powered Stearman owned by Tim Lyons, and '26' pass Ely Cathedral *en route* to a show at the historic Shuttleworth Collection at Old Warden in the summer of 1995. In July each year Stearmans from all over Britain converge on the famous Bedfordshire airfield for the annual Arnold Register Day. (*Martin Bowman*)

Such has been the enthusiasm, there are literally hundreds of airworthy Stearmans on civil air registers around the world. Scores of dedicated Stearman owners, restorers and potential restorers belong to the Stearman Restorers Association which has members scattered throughout the USA, Europe, South America, and the southern hemisphere (see page 151 for more information). All are proud of the Stearman's longevity and its distinguished history. *(Martin Bowman)*

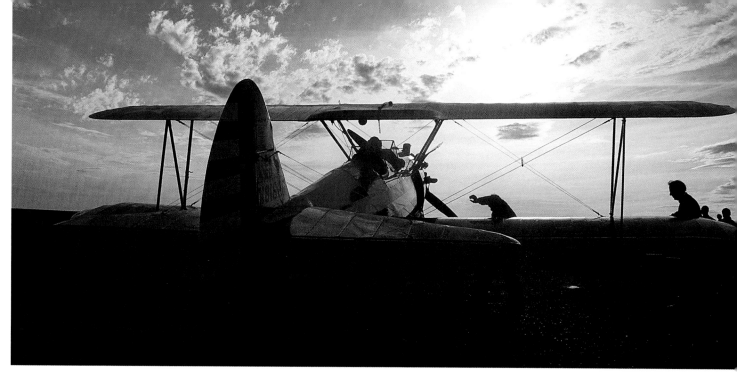

Stearman at sunset.
(*Martin Bowman*)

Bolivian Stearman FAB-007 on display at the Bolivian Air Force Academy at Santa Cruz in October 1994. The Bolivian Air Force was supplied with five A75N1/PT-17 aircraft (c/n 75-3334–3338) between July and September 1942 and a further five E75N1/N2S-4s in 1943 (75-3446–3450) under the Lend-Lease scheme. Further ex-US Army and Navy Stearmans were also purchased after WWII by several other South American countries, including Nicaragua (six PT-13s in 1948) and Guatemala (1951). In 1945, Lt-Col Malcolm Stewart went on a buying spree for the Honduran Air Force. His purchases included six PT-17s, four of them powered by R-670s, and two Wasp Jnr engined models, but on delivery from Miami in February 1946, four of the PT-17s were forced down during a storm at Matanzas, Cuba, and three were destroyed. In June 1948, against the advice of Lt-Col Stewart, 12 PT-13s were acquired in a deal set up by Sn Andreas Rodriguez, a Government official. These aircraft were little used and by July, three were scrapped for spares. In April 1948 15 PT-13s and PT-17s were acquired by the Dominican Republic from a Florida brokers and by November, 32 were on strength. By January 1950 only 22 remained as these were serialled, 1301/1321. These remained in service until 1957. El Salvador, meanwhile, had acquired 8 Stearmans 1951–56, including, N5474N, N50490, N52108, N54652 and N64931. Air Force pilots used the aircraft as crop dusters to increase flying hours and for additional training. (*Graham Dinsdale*)

6. Wing Nuts and Aerobatics

Some of the dusters and other old stagers refused to trade in their tail draggers for tricycle-geared Cessnas and Beechcraft and earned a few bucks with barnstorming and wing-walking acts at rodeos and country fairs on blissful holiday weekends. The Model 75's big beefy shape, fat tyres, strong undercarriage, and big bluff engine and its almost viceless, stable handling characteristics, make it an ideal training aircraft. But this does put limitations on its aerobatic prowess. However, with a few enhancements and modifications – the stock 220hp engine is normally replaced by the powerful 450hp Wasp, a pair of ailerons are added to the top wing and an unforgettable colour scheme is applied to complete its metamorphosis – the Stearman is transformed into a star aerobatic performer. The only other concessions are smoke generation and, of course, an upper wing bracing and a stanchion for the wing walker.

Stearmans, of course, have been used in Hollywood movies since the days of Paul Mantz, and so too have they been used for barnstorming, aerobatics and wing walking. Vic Norman, who likes to describe himself as a young, modern-day barnstormer and entertainer, is the pilot of one of three 450hp Stearmans *avec* young lady standing on top of the forty-six US gallon fuel tank and bolted between the upper planes of my hard-working biplane'. 'Responsibility,' he says, 'starts here.'

Vic started flying in 1965 and has done over 1,500 public displays. His brainchild, and undoubtedly Britain's most famous wing walk act, is his Rencombe, Gloucestershire-based Aerosuperbatics Ltd, better known to the public as Cadbury's Crunchie Flying Circus. Norman says that the trouble with the British air display scene is that it is all so serious and most people forget that it is the public that pays to be entertained. In 1990 he used his experience to develop the circus into a barnstorming performance to excite and captivate his audience. He says, 'I spend hours trying to develop new ideas to build into our display and test everything out myself first-hand. When I'm happy the team perfects our ideas and incorporates them into the display. I would hate to ever become boring, and hope to become old.'

No one could ever accuse Norman of being boring. He says: 'In the twenties of course, the flying daredevils rode the wild wind. Barnstorming! The most famous of all was probably Earl Dougherty, whose spectacular wing-walker stunts lured his passengers to the airfield for rides at so many bucks a go. Daredevil Lindbergh was one of the early wing walkers and an expert parachute jumper who on the odd occasion took to the silk rather than press on in bad weather. Girls had their fair share of excitement too, such as Princess Elly Jonescu, a Romanian beauty and multi-linguist, who found life in her homeland boring. 'My favourite was Ethel Dare, the flying witch (I've named my dog after her), real name Margie Hobbs. She did ninety-six plane changes in the twenties before retiring. This pretty teenager was the first to jump out on to the bottom wing of her Jenny, scamper along and swing herself up on to another machine flying alongside and slightly overhead. Today, of course, the restrictions of the CAA and the FAA mean whatever feats we perform are mega-safe compared with those true daredevils. But I'm often asked what it's like to fly the Stearman with someone strapped on top . . .

124

One of the most famous pairings of man and Stearman was Englishman John Jordan and his airplane; born 1921, heir to the Jordan family at Biggleswade, Bedfordshire, millers since 1855. Jordan's love of flying and the thrill of the throttle began at the age of nine when neighbour Richard Shuttleworth, collector of aircraft and cars, took him aloft in a Tiger Moth. In WWII Jordan flew with the RAF, served in the ATA, and tested Spitfires, 'spending more time upside down than the right way up'. 'Dead easy,' he recalls, 'but then one day we started discussing whether you could aerobat a bomber.' Jordan could and did, flying a Warwick inverted during ten slow rolls! After the war Jordan turned to dusting in California flying the Stearman. Every night he washed the back out to clear the acid after seeing one tail fall off. In 1961 Jordan started up the

first aerial spraying company in the UK using the same Fleetways Stearman. He carried on a very successful crop spraying business until 1972, when there was 'no mould, no crop disease, no aphids, no nothing. Everything was just bursting with bloody health.' He sold everything, except the Stearman. Movie companies contracted him to fly thrilling sequences for the *Battle of Britain, Those Magnificent Men in Their Flying Machines* and *The Aviator*. In *Biggles* (pictured) he appeared with his Stearman, bedecked with the Iron Cross, as von Stalheim in a series of set pieces with Mike Peare. A motorist once took Jordan to court for flying 20ft above his head. 'What did he expect,' says Jordan, 'if he parked his car at the end of the runway? He said he didn't expect me to be flying upside down.'

'Before we start, I like to walk out towards the machine drawn up in beautiful alignment in front of the shed. It makes me feel very lucky and privileged to be able to fly such a beautiful big biplane. After normal pre-flight inspection (fuel and oil and other boring things) we pull Mr Pratt & Whitney through eighteen blades slowly. This allows oil in the bottom cylinders to work its way past the exhaust valves into the exhaust and no longer puts any load on the cylinder head studs. Then we get the wing riders on top, not an easy job first time round: hopping on to the bottom wing walkway then on to the front seat and cockpit slides, a foot on the bottom of the front windshield, a big pull up through the wires on to the wing rack, feet into the footwells and leather straps (only soft-soled shoes allowed) and finally doing up the "Jack Hooker" specially built straps/harness. This has a very clever little safety pin as a double check that your rider is really secure. The straps must be tight for aerobatic flight.

'The pilot then straps himself in, checks that the girl/rider is all done up by getting the positive reply "belts secure and locked". If we are taking a stranger, we do up their belts for them, leaving nothing to chance. Then the normal "Clear Prop" and engine start. The girl makes a visual check and gives the standard start signal and the big Pratt & Whitney coughs into life, emitting much smoke if it's the first start of the day, as the oil in the exhaust is burnt, and assuming of course that you have remembered to prime the old girl. The engine then settles down to a throaty rumble warming up at 800 rpm looking for an oil temperature of 20° before taxying. You are aware of the spacious cockpit where everything is easily adjustable – I normally put the seat right down in an attempt to keep warm. The rudder pedals are adjustable over a range of about a foot fore and aft. This aeroplane can really be flown in comfort by very large pilots.

Bob and Pat Wagner, a husband and wife wing-walking team, who have been married for over twenty years, have been performing together in air shows in N450PW since 1971. In 1982 they purchased their own airport – Wagner International in Ohio. Pat holds a commercial certificate in single-engine land and seaplanes and gliders. (*Via Jim Koepnick, EAA*)

Well known on the American air show circuit for many years is wing-walker Ruthie Blankenship and her pilot and husband, Southwest Airlines pilot Bob. Ruthie also holds a private pilot's licence. Up until 1994 they operated their 450hp Boeing Stearman Special *Ole Red* at air shows throughout the USA. *Ole Red* is now owned by Susan Dacy. In 1995 Susan became the first female to fly a Stearman in air shows. (*Via Dick Knapinski, EAA*)

'The chocks are jerked out and we start taxying with particular caution; you must first check that your way ahead is clear and exactly how your wheels are going to travel. Although the Stearman is tail-heavy on the ground, you just can't take a chance of nosing over and the girl is also briefed to keep a good lookout while waving at the crowd – so a lot of weaving and rubber-necking is needed. Standard run-up and pre-flight checks are carried out plus a positive thumbs-up from the wing rider just before take-off. No real trouble during take-off: steady application of power (we use only thirty inches of manifold pressure although you can go up to thirty-six – but there is just no need). The motor makes a glorious deep powerful note, sweet and clear; there are no worries about a false note. The tail comes up after about twenty yards' ground run. Her speed goes faster and faster then, whoops, she lifts herself off the ground. Directional control is very positive but quite big movements of the rudder can be required plus a certain amount of speed with the feet – no jet jockeys here.

'At around 60 mph the big old girl flies herself off the ground and would climb at a very respectable rate. But today we have an air display to do and by the time we are at the end of the crowd line, I pull up and away from the crowd turning that excess speed of 40-odd mph into height and fly a low G turn back on to the display line, gently losing height back down to my lower limit of 30ft while taking off the power and flying a big side-slip, cross-controlling, keeping the speed as low as possible to enable the wing rider to do her thing – wave, take a leg out and whatever else turns her on. It's strange, but with a girl on the wing I am always trying to fly as slowly as possible to keep manoeuvres comfortable for my wing rider. I am told that at 100 mph plus it gets very hard to wave and that between 70 and 80 it's just great.

'Now it's maximum everything: 2,100 rpm, thirty-six inches of manifold pressure and a spiral climb in front of the crowd, those 450 horses cutting away, hauling us to the heavens. Soon we are at 1,500ft and now diving crowd centre, picking up speed like a flying brick – 135 mph and gently in the loop followed by other basic aeros but all so gently.

'I am now in position for the interesting bit: lining up for the inverted fly-by, or, if I were in formation, the mirror, wiggle, wiggle. Helen [Tempest] gives me the thumbs-up, diving to 250ft above ground level, 125 mph, pull the nose well up, unload the stick and roll. A gentle push forward on the stick, the speed settles to 100 mph and I am now up and the brave lass is down, upside down and, can you believe, still waving.

'Some people have asked why not do it lower than 250ft. I'll tell you why, because I checked it out. If you are the wrong way up with Madame Drag on top and the engine fails, you need 250ft to dive, roll out and land. Well, that bit of fun done, it's back to the low-level barnstorming: big waving, zig-zagging, zagging, upping and downing, wagging your rear end, all not above 80 mph or the crew can't do her thing, getting your leg out, blowing chocolate kisses . . .

'Now the bit that any good Stearman pilot never takes for granted. It's no problem getting over the numbers, a bit of side-slip on at 80 mph, kicking off the drift, rounding out, noting what the wind is doing and gently touching down, but keeping her running on the straight and narrow needs all one's faculties, or in that famous old airman's saying: "If your machine one day starts veering against the course that you are steering, don't make a grouse of it or say your bird has got a twist that way. Admit what's certain to be true – the twist, dear pilot, lies in you. You can always find a big surprise waiting where you least surmise." '

Cheryl Rae Littlefield, a native of Chicago, is a licensed pilot and wing walker, one of only ten wing walkers in the world. She walks the wing on husband Gene's *The Littlefield Scheunemann Special*, radio call sign 'Magic One', a 1942-built, ex-Venezuelan and Guatemalan-owned A75N1, highly modified for air shows by Les Schueneman to include a Pratt & Whitney engine, four ailerons and inverted fuel and smoke. Cheryl's speciality is to 'disappear' while moving around the aircraft from the top wing to the lower wing. Gene has been flying for over twenty-five years and over 4,000 hours. He holds several ratings and has flown over a hundred different types of aircraft. Cheryl wanted to become a wing walker after seeing a newscaster ride the wing of Gene's Stearman to promote a local air show. They met through a mutual friend in 1981, later married, and now live in Plainfield, Illinois where they run 'Gene Littlefield Air Shows' and a school of aerobatics. *(Jim Koepnick, EAA)*

Bob Barden performing in *Black Baron* at Ann Arbor, Mi, HQ for his ACRO – Airshow Company Recruiting Office. Barden, 6ft 2in and 185lb, had been a pilot and aviation enthusiast for many years when in 1972 he was offered a ride in a Stearman by an old friend. Barden has been on the air show scene since 1978 and is the recipient of many awards. He can provide one or all of a dozen routines including rope ladder, car to plane change, wing-walking act, opening flag jumper, and biplanes circling the jumper, as well as professional air show announcer and landing a Cub on a speeding pick-up truck. The *Black Baron* was built in 1941 with a 220hp engine, was restored in 1966 and highly modified with a 450hp engine, four ailerons and a smoke generation system. What makes Bob's remarkable act that little bit different is that his wing-walking stuntman is Eddie 'The Grip' Green, a Ford Motor Co. executive from Pinckney. He has over 1,100 trips atop an aircraft, 1,190 car to plane transfers and in 1975 in Toronto, Canada was the first person to accomplish a boat to plane transfer. Eddie is also a skydiving champion and has made 2,550 parachute jumps, some of which include the air show opening flag jump. *(Bob Barden)*

(right)
Eddie Andreini's aeronautical repertoire includes opening air shows with a stunt he has performed many times. At Redding Municipal airport in July 1995 two men held a ribbon between two poles ten feet off the ground and on his second pass Andreini flew inverted and cut the ribbon with his tailplane! The ribbon holders did not have the same faith in Andreini's flying ability – they dropped the pole and ran for their lives!

Girls who like to wing-walk have to be no more than 5ft 6in in height and enjoy travelling at speeds of up to 180 mph strapped to the top wing! Susan King, thirty-seven-year-old mother and legal secretary, 5ft 5in tall and weighing 125lb, wanted to be a wing walker after seeing another woman do a wing-walking act for the Flying Circus in Bealeton, Virginia in 1980. She hoped her Stearman owner dad, John, sixty-two, a twenty-year veteran of Navy flying and former flight school instructor for an airline, would agree, but he said, 'Not on your life will my daughter be out on the wing of a plane.' Susan, however, was determined. She learned to skydive and in the summer of 1985 began building up her strength at a local spa, while taking lessons from another wing-walker at the Flying Circus. Her enthusiasm and determination were such that her father relented, and they began performing together in what was the only father-daughter wing-walking team in the world. Susan King says that wing-walking is like mountain climbing, with the key being to take one step at a time. 'I'm always frightened,' she said. 'If you're not scared, you're not safe. I don't feel or think anything else when I'm up there.'

Wing-walking has a relatively good safety record but regulations change every year in aviation. In the USA the wing-walker may climb all over the aircraft but may not fly between the airfield and the display site attached to the rig. In Sweden, the wing-walker must return to her seat inside the aircraft for landing. Anyone who believes that aerobatics, and in particular the sport of wing-walking, is a glamorous, exhilirating profession for competitive and fearless men and women, they would be right. Standing on the wing of a Stearman while it flies inverted is not for faint-hearted mortals. Neither is piloting an aerobatic aircraft through a mind-spinning, heart-stopping, multiple G manoeuvres, for once in the air the Stearman pilots take their wing-walkers through loops, rolls and hammerhead stalls. Hopefully, the public will be treated to these displays as long as there are aircraft to fly and wing-walkers daring to perch upon them.

It's one thing to want to ride in a 450hp 'Super Stearman'; it's another to want to fly it. But it's hard to imagine anyone wanting to crawl all over it during flight, and then jump off! Veteran skydiver Alan Silver, who has performed more than 2,400 jumps in thirty years, does. His pilot is Eddie Andreini, a twenty-year veteran aerobatic pilot. They teamed up in 1990 to put together one of the best new acts on the air show circuit. Andreini performs his tight, high-energy aerobatic routine while Silver is cavorting on the wings, in the wires and in the specially designed rack on top of the roaring Stearman. After some of the most breathtaking manoeuvres ever performed by man and machine, and a final inverted pass, Andreini and Silver zoom skyward and Silver does the world's highest swan dive. The two are seen here performing near the Golden Gate, San Francisco. *(Eddie Andreini)*

(right)
In 1979, the Red Baron Stearman Squadron began barnstorming in the USA. Flying nine months of the year, they have raised millions of dollars for children's charities. The Squadron, which is based at Ryan Field, Marshall, Minnesota, began performing at air shows in 1984 and has won awards for professionalism and showmanship. Each of the six 'Super Stearmans', all of which have been restored to a standard configuration and modified using 450hp Wasp Jr engines, and fuel and oil systems to allow the aircraft to fly inverted, is flown in excess of 600 hours per year by a pool of eleven pilots. An additional set of ailerons increases the aircraft's roll rate; wheel pants and engine cowling have been added to cut drag. Smoke systems have been installed to trace the path of the planes through the sky. *(Red Baron Stearman Squadron)*

Stearman

N2S-3 75-1180 in US Navy 'yellow peril' scheme in the hands of Stearman Display Team pilot Bruce Monk, entering a loop 1,500ft over Norfolk, England in 1992. As a Squadron Leader, RAF, Monk flew more than 6,000 hours on Hawker Hunters, Harriers and Tornados and was Harrier display pilot at Wildenrath in 1975 and the RAF Germany Tornado display pilot for the 1986 display season. He is now a Line Training Captain on the Fokker F100 for Air UK out of Stansted. Describing the loop, he says: 'Full power and wing-over left to clear the area and align with the line feature. Continuing the wing-over into a dive, check both wings level with speed approaching 120 mph, slightly back on the throttle to maintain red line revs and smoothly back on the stick to 4G full power again as the nose comes up. Ease off the stick pressure as the nose passes 60° of pitch to achieve a round loop and now check wings level. Now head back over the top with the world upside down, and the line feature coming into view the stick is eased off further as we float over the top of the loop. As the nose drops over the top and speed increases the back pressure on the stick is increased, throttle reduced slightly as rpm builds to achieve the same height and speed as the entry. Bump! It is satisfying to fly through your own slipstream. I wonder if I could have done a better loop if I had remembered to put the slip ball in the middle before pulling up?' *(Steve Jefferson)*

134

Britain's most famous wing-walk act is Aerosuperbatics Ltd, better known to the public as Cadbury's Crunchie Flying Circus. They make a unique formation team with smoke-generating 450hp Pratt & Whitney-powered gold and orange Stearmans, each with a glamorous wing-walker flying on the top wing. Flying at heights of between 30ft and 2,000ft, the Crunchies perform a range of aerobatic manoeuvres, including mirror formations, rolls and loops. The team holds three world records: the shortest distance aerial baton pass; the world wing-walking endurance record; and the world's youngest ever wing-walker, Sam Norman, aged fourteen. When one of the wing-walking positions became vacant in 1991, the team was inundated with over 2,000 young girl applicants. Twenty-one-year-old Sarah Cubitt was the girl finally selected from a shortlist of six drawn up by Helen Tempest and two Red Arrows pilots from the legions of hopefuls. *(Bob Holder)*

(left and right)
Standing on the wing of a Stearman while it flies inverted is not for the faint-hearted. Neither is piloting an aerobatic aircraft through a mind-spinning, heart-stopping, multiple-G manoeuvre, for once in the air the Stearman pilots take their wing-walkers through loops, rolls and hammerhead stalls. Here, Helen Tempest, is dramatically photographed on a Crunchie Flying Circus Stearman. *(Courtesy Vic Norman)*

Helen Tempest, born 1968, from King's Cliffe, near Peterborough, was Britain's youngest wing-walker when, aged 15, she first flew on the wing of a Tiger Moth piloted by father Barry Tempest. She has been wing-walking since 1983, and retired in January 1997.
(Martin Bowman)

Construction/Registration Numbers

Model	C/No	Reg/No	Details
C-1	101 11a	NR3741	
C-1	101 11b	NR4100	
C-2	102	NR1682	
C-2M	103	NR1598	Nat Parks
C-3D	104	NR3440	

Model	C/No	Reg/No	Details
C-3A	113		
C-3A	115	NR4552	
C-3B	105	NR3709	Western Air Express crash.7 May 29
C-3BSP	106	NR3863	Western Air Express crash.10 Aug 30
C-3B	107	NR3922	
C3MB	108	NR4011	No.202
C-3K (C-2K)	109	NR4098	128hp Ryan-Siemens-Halske SH12 engine

Model	C/No	Reg/No	Details
C-3B	110	NR4099	
C-3MB	111	NR4273	
C-3B	112	NR4274	
C-3MB	114	NR5500	
C-3B	116	NR4703	
C-3K (C-2K)	117	NR4713	128hp Ryan-Siemens-Halske SH12 engine
C-3B	118	NR4714	
C-3B	119	NR4715	
C-3B	120	NR4716	
C-3B	121	NC5415	Alaska Aviation Heritage Mus., Anchorage
C-3H	122	NR5600	
C-3B	123	NR5084	
C-3B	124	NR5085	
C-3B	125	NR5308	
C-3B	126	NR7550/NR5309	Mus of Flt, Seattle, Wash.
C-3B	127	NR5310	
C-3B	128	NR5489	
C-3B	129	NR5490	
C-3B	130	NR5491	
C-3B	131	NR5685	
C-3B	132	NR5686	
C-3B	133	NR5687	
C-3B	134	G-CARR	(Canadian)
C-3B	135	NR6101	
C-3B	136	NR6102	
C-3K (C-2K)	137	NR	Delivered as fuselage only.
C-3MB	138	NR7171	
C-3B	139	NR6432	
C-3B	140	NR6154	
C-3D	141	NR6157	
C-3B	142	NR6252	
C-3B	143	NR6158	
C-3B	144	NR6253	Texas Dusting Co./Delta Air Services
C-3B	145	NR6250	
C-3B	146	NR6159	
C-3B	147	NR6254	
C-3B	148	NR6251	
C-3B	150	NR6256	
C-3B	151	NR6255	
C-3B	152	NR6257	
C-3B	153	NS??17	
C-3B	154	NR6409	
C-3B	155	NR6258	
C-3B	156	NR6259	
C-3B	157	NR9062	
C-3B	158	NR6153	
C-3B	159	NR6260	
C-3MB	160	NR6261	
C-3B	161	NR6411	
C-3B	162	NR6412	
C-3B	163	NR7547	
C-3B	164	NR7548	
C-3B	165	NR7549	
C-3B	166	NR7550	Delta Air Services
C-3B	167	NR6407	
C-3B	168	NR6408	
C-3L(C-3B)	169	X-6438	Re-engined with 130hp Comet, 7/10/28.
C-3B	170	NR6410	
C-3B	171	NR6431	
C-3MB	172	NR6486	National Parks
C-3B/D	173	NR6433	

Model	C/No	Reg/No	Details
C-3B	174	NR6434	
C-3B	175	NR6435	
C-3B	176	NR6436	
C-3B	177	NR6437	
C-3MB	178	NR6487	13/10/38. National Parks; Johnson Flying Service
C-3B	179	NR6439	
C-3B	180	NR6440	
C-3B	181	NR6481	
C-3B	182	NR6482	
C-3B	183	NR6483	
C-3B	184	NR6484	
C-3B	185	NR6488	
C-3B	186	NR6489	
C-3B	187	NR6485	
C-3MB	188	NR6490	
C-3B	189	NR6492	
C-3B	190	NR6491	
C-3B	191	NR6493	
C-3B	192	NR6494	
C-3B	193	NR6495	Western Air Express. 15/12/28
C-3B	194	NR6497	
C-3B	195	NR6499	
C-3B	196	NR6498	
C-3B	197	NR9056	
C-3B	200	NR9065	
C-3MB	201	NR9058	
C-3B	202	NR6155	
C-3B	203	NR9066	
C-3B	204	NR9067	
C-3MB	205	NC9057	
C-3B	206	NC9064	
C-3MB	207	NR6496	Texas Dusting Co; Delta Air Service; Airworthy. D. Blankenbaker
C-3B	208	NS??18	
C-3B	209	NC9068	
C-3MB	210	NC9059	
C-3MB	211	NC9060	
C-3MB	212	NC9061	
C-3B	213	NC9069	
C-3B	214	NR8197	
C-3B	215	NR8198	
C-3B	216	NR8801	
C-3B	217	NR8807	
C-3B	218	NR8806	
C-3B	219	NR8809	Ross Hadley
C-3B	220	NR8812	
C-3B	221	NR8811	
C-3B	222	NR8802	
C-3B	223	NR8803	
C-3B	224	NR8804	
C-3B	225	NR8805	
C-3B	226	NR8810	
C-3B	227	NR8813	Texas Dusting Co/Delta Air Service
C-3B	228	NR8814	Delta Air Service
C-3B	229	NC8815	Western Air Express F/N 206
C-3B	230	NC8816	
C-3B	231	NC8817	
C-3B	232	NC8818	6 May 28 Nat Parks/Nick Mamer 7 Sept 34
C-3B	233	NS?22?	
C-3B	234	NC8819	
C-3B	235	NC8820	17 May 29 WAE. Crash.6 Jan 30, Denver, Co
C-3B	236	NC8821	

Model	C/No	Reg/No	Details
C-3B	237	NC8823	
C-3B	237A	N?23	
C-3B	238	NC8824	
C-3B	239	NC8825	
C-3B	240	NC8826	
C-3B	241	NC8835	(Airworthy 85)
C-3B	242	NC8836	
C-3B	243	NC8838	
C-3B	244	NC8830	
C-3B	245	NC8831	
C-3B	246	NC8834	
C-3B	247	NC8837	
C-3B	248	NR882N	R. Halliburton 'The Flying Carpet'
C-3R	5001	NC8828	Historical Aircraft Restoration Mus. Maryland Heights
C-3R	5002	NC8822	20/11/35. Chicago Southern Airlines.
C-3R	5003	NC8840	
C-3R	5004	NC659K	Shell Oil
C-3R	5005	NC657K	
C-3R	5006	NC658K	
C-3R	5007	NC656K	Airworthy
C-3R	5008	NC660K	
C-3R	5009	NC661K	
C-3R	5010	NC662K	
C-3R	5011	NC668K	
C-3R	5012	NC669K	
C-3R	5013	NC670K	
C-3R	5014	NC671K	
C-3R	5015	NC672K	
C-3R	5016	NC673K	
C-3R	5017	NC675K	
C-3R	5018	NC773H	
C-3R	5019	NC775H	(to 4DM)
C-3R	5020–5029		10 a/c for Peruvian Air Force
C-3R	5030	NC780H	
C-3R	5031	NC781H	
C-3R	5032	NC782H	
C-3R	5033	NC782H	
C-3R	5034	NC790H	
C-3R	5035	NC793H	
C-3R	5036	NC794H	Jeff Robinson
C-3R	5037	NC799H	Dick McWhorter
C-3P	5039	NC587Y	
M-2	1001	NC9051	To Varney
M-2	1002	NC9052	To Varney
M-2	1003	NC9053	To Varney
M-2	1004	NC9054	To Varney
M-2	1005	NC9055	To Varney
M-2	1006	NC8199	
M-2	1007	NC8827	To Varney
LT-1	2001	NC8829	
LT-1	2002	NC8832	
LT-1	2003	NC8833	
CAB-1 'Coach'	3001	X-8808	
4C	4001	NC2	
4C	4002	NC8839	
4C	4003	NC665K	
4E	4004	NC664K	
4E	4005	NC663K	William Ben Scott, Reno, NV
4E	4006	NC666K	
4C	4007	NC667K	
4E	4008	NC674K	

Model	C/No	Reg/No	Details
4D	4009	NC769H	
4CM	4010	NC770H	C'vtd to 4EM. Western Canada Aviation Mus, (CF-ASF) Winnipeg MB
4DM	4011	NC774H	Delivered to Western Air Express as a 4D
4CM	4012	NC772H	Converted to 4EM
4CM	4013	CF-CCG	Converted to 4EM
4C	4014	CF-BSQ	Converted to 4DM
4D	4015	NC776H	
4EM	4016	CF-AMB	Canadian
4EM	4017		Canadian
4C	4018	NC778H	
4E	4019	NC779H	Airworthy, Blakeberg 85
4E	4020		
4E (Special)	4021	NC784H	STD Oil CF-AMB Nat A'nautical Coll. Rockliffe, Ont. 10/7/30.
4E (Special)	4022	NC785H	Standard Oil of California. 10/7/30.
4E	4023	NC791H	Airpower Museum, Ottumwa IA.
4D	4024		
4D	4025	NC796H	Carol and Ron Rex, Leeward Ranch, Fl.
4D	4026	N11724	Yankee Air Museum, Chino CA.
4D	4027	NC563Y	
4EM	4028		Canadian
4CM-1	4030	NC482W	
4CM-1	4031	NC483W	Temp. test bed for Ranger V-770 (4CM-1)
4CM-1	4032	NC484W	
4CM-1	4033	NC485W	Owned & flown by Addison Pemberton, Spokane, Wash.
4CM-1	4034	NC486W	
4CM-1	4035	NC487W	24 Oct 35. American Airlines. Wrecked in emergency landing, Franconia, Va.
4CM-1	4036	NC488W	
4CM-1	4037	NC489W	
4CM-1	4038	NC490W	20 Jan 33. American Airlines. 1 Mail flt crashed in fog, Little Kennesaw Mt, Marietta, Ga.
4CM-1	4039	NC11721	20 Jan 33. American Airlines. 1 Mail Flight struck hill, crashed, Dallas-Brownsville mail route near Bourne
4CM-1	4040	NC783H	C'vtd to 2-place 4EX with 450bhp supercharged Wasp for Standard Oil Co.
4CM-1	4041		

Model	C/No	Reg/Army/Navy Serial No.	Notes
6A	6001	786H	6D (YBT-5), 6H, 6L
6P	6002	NX787H	Fitted with 220 bhp Wright J-5
6F	6003	NC788H/N788H	Am Aero Foundation Mus, Westlake Village, Richmond CA (Mod. to 6L)
6A	6004	N795H	Yankee Air Museum, Chino, CA
YPT-9 (6A)	6005	31-460	Converted to YPT-9B with Lycoming R-680
YPT-9 (6A)	6006	31-461	YBT-3 basic trainer/YPT-9C (6H) Lycoming R-680
YPT-9 (6A)	6007	31-462	Fitted with R-985-1 to become YBT-5 (6D)
YPT-9 (6A)	6008	31-459	Converted to YPT-9B (6L) with Lycoming R-680
6H	6009	NC564Y	
6C (YBT-3)	6010	NC2143	
70/XPT-943	70-000	X571Y	US Navy
X75/X75L3	75-000	X-14407	Tested by AAC with 225bhp Wright R-760E and as XL5L3 by US Navy with a military Lycoming R-680-3. Re-engined with Commercial R-680B4B and sold in April 1937 to a private owner
73 (NS-1)	73-001-041	9677-9717	First US Navy order for 40 aircraft
73 (NS-1)	73-042-061	0191-0210	Second US Navy order for 20 aircraft
73L1	73-062-068		7 a/c to Philippine Govt with Navy Lycoming R-680-4.
A73L3	73-069-071		3 a/c to Philippine Govt with Navy Lycoming R-680C-1 engines
A73B1	73-072-078		7 aircraft to Cuban Government 1939–1940

Model	C/No	Reg/No	Details
75 (PT-13)	75-001/026	36-2/27	26 a/c
A75 (PT-13A)	75-027/070	37-71/114	44 a/c
A75 (PT-13A)	75-071/098	37-232/259	28 a/c
A75 (PT-13A)	75-099/118	38-451/470	20 a/c
A75 (PT-13A)	75-119/298	40-1562/1741	180 a/c (40-1620 cv. to PT-13C)
A75 (PT-17)	75-299/448	40-1742/1891	150 a/c
A75J1 (PT-18–18A)	75-449/598	40-1892/2041	150 a/c. Jacobs R-755-7 engine. Six equipped for night & instrument flying. (40-1906, 09, 34 to PT-18A)
A75L3	75-599/618		20 a/c loan to Brazil
A75L3	75-619/621		3 a/c loan to Venezuela
A75N1 (PT-17)	75-622/846	41-862/1086	225 a/c
A75 (PT-13B)	75-847/291	41-787/861	75 a/c (41-853 cv. to PT-13C)
A75N1 (N2S-1)	75-922/999	3145/3222	78 a/c (orig. 600-1. Dv to 2/3)
A75N1 (N2S-1)	75-1000/1171	3223/3394	172 a/c
B75N1 (N2S-3)	75-1172/1296	3395/3519	125 a/c
B75 (N2S-2)	75-1297/1421	3520/3644	125 a/c. Lycoming R-680-8.
A75L3	75-1422/1425	NC32496/32499	4 a/c to Parks Air College
A75N1 (PT-17)	75-1426/2569	41-7867/9010	1144 a/c (12 cv. to PT-17A)
A75L3	75-2570/2581		12 a/c loan to Philippine Govt
B75N1 (N2S-3)	75-2582/2681	4252/4351	100 a/c
A75B4	75-2682-2686		5 a/c to Venezuela with 320bhp Wright R-760E2 & wing arm
A75L3	75-2687/2690		4 a/c loan to Venezuela
A75N1 (PT-17)	75-2691/2812	41-25202/25323	122 a/c (3 cv. to PT-17B dusters)
A75N1	75-2813/2818		6 a/c loan to Peru
A75N1 (PT-17)	75-2819/2878	41-25324/25383	60 a/c
A75N1	75-2879/2884		6 a/c loan to Peru
A75N1 (PT-17)	75-2885/2968	41-25384/25467	84 a/c
A75N1	75-2969/2974		6 a/c loan to Peru
A75N1 (PT-17)	75-2975/3233	41-25468/25726	259 a/c
A75N1 (N2S-4)	75-3234/3248	27960/27974	15 a/c with R-670-5 diverted from Army PT-17 order ex41-25802/25816
A75N1 (PT-17)	75-3249	41-25742	1 a/c
A75N1 (N2S-4)	75-3250/3333	27975/28058	84 a/c with R-670-5 diverted from Army PT-17 order ex41-25817/25900
A75N1 (PT-17)	75-3334/3338	41-25727/25731	5 a/c on loan to Bolivia
A75N1 (PT-17)	75-3339/3343	41-25732/25736	5 a/c loan to Paraguay
A75N1 (N2S-4)	75-3344/3347	30014/30017	4 a/c. R-680-4 (orig. PT-17A 41-25737/41-25740) ex 41-25992/25995
A75N1 (PT-17A)	75-3348	41-25741	Loan to Cuba
A75N1 (PT-17A)	75-3349/3353	41-25743/25747	5 a/c loan to Cuba
A75N1 (N2S-4)	75-3354/3404	29923/29973	51 a/c ex 41-25901/25951
A75N1 (N2S-4)	75-3405	30018	1 a/c ex 41-259996
A75N1 (N2S-4)	75-3406/3444	29975/30013	39 a/c ex 41-25953/25991
A75N1 (N2S-4)	75-3445	29974	1 a/c ex 41-25952
A75N1 (N2S-4)	75-3446/3450	34097/34101	5 a/c ex 41-25737/25740, 25748
A75N1 (PT-17A)	75-3451/3455	41-25749/25753	5 a/c loan to Paraguay
A75N1 (N2S-4)	75-3456/3491	30019/30054	36 a/c ex 41-25997/26032
A75N1 (PT-17A)	75-3492/3493	41-25754/25755	2 a/c loan to Columbia
A75N1 (N2S-4)	75-3494/3565	30055/30126	72 a/c ex 41-26033/26104. Orig. intended as loan to Bolivia
A75N1 (PT-17)	75-3566/3569	41-25756/25759	4 a/c loan to Columbia
A75N1 (PT-17)	75-3570/3577	41-25760/25767	8 a/c
A75N1 (N2S-4)	75-3578/3580	34107/34109	3 a/c ex 41-26125/26127. Bu 34102/34106 canc. from orig. block 34102/34111
A75N1 (N2S-4)	75-3581/3600	30127/30146	20 a/c ex 41-26105/26124
A75N1 (N2S-4)	75-3601/3602	34110/34111	2 a/c ex 41-26128/26129
A75N1 (N2S-4) (AL75L5)	75-3603/3714	37856/37967	112 a/c (37901/753648 rebuilt & fitted with 190bhp Lycoming 0-435-11 for Rep of China in 1947) ex 41-26130/26241
A75N1 (N2S-4)	75-3715/3724	37978/37987	10 a/c ex 41-26242/26251. Orig. Ltr. Int for 1200 N2S-3
A75N1 (PT-17) (N2S-4)	75-3725/3758	41-25768/25801	34 a/c 450 PT-17, 41-25802/26251, cancelled from orig. contract. Became N2S-4.
D75N1 (PT-27)	75-3759/3790	42-15570/15601	32 a/c for RCAF FD968/999
D75N1 (PT-27)	75-3791/4014	42-15602/15825	224 a/c for RCAF FJ741/964
D75N1 (PT-27)	75-4015/4031	42-15826/15842	17 a/c for RCAF FJ965/981
D75N1 (PT-27)	75-4032/4049	42-15843/15860	18 a/c for RCAF FJ982/999

Model	C/No	Reg/No	Details
D75N1 (PT-27)	75-4050/4057	42-15861/15868	8 a/c for RCAF FK100/107
D75N1 (PT-27)	75-4058Special	42-15869	1 a/c FK108 for RCAF (with enclosed canopy)
A75N1 (PT-17)	75-4059/4208	42-15896/16045	150 a/c loan to China
A75N1 (PT-17)	75-4029/4436	42-16046/16273	228 a/c
A75N1 (PT-17)	75-4437/4439	42-16274/16726	3 a/c loan for Cuba
A75N1 (PT-17)	75-4440/4537	42-16277/16374	98 a/c
A75N1 (PT-17)	75-4538/4539	42-16375/16376	2 a/c loan Guatemala
A75N1 (PT-17)	75-4540/4657	42-16377/16494	118 a/c
A75N1 (PT-17)	75-4658/4660	42-16495/16497	3 a/c loan to Colombia
A75N1 (PT-17)	75-4661/4807	42-16498/16644	147 a/c
A75N1 (PT-17)	75-4808/4810	42-16645/16647	3 a/c loan to Colombia
A75N1 (PT-17)	75-4811/4813	42-16648/16650	3 a/c loan to Dominica
A75N1 (PT-17)	75-4814/4880	42-16651/16717	67 a/c
A75N1 (PT-17)	75-4881/4886	42-16718/16723	6 a/c loan to Colombia
A75N1 (N2S-4)	75-4887/5008	55650/55771	122 a/c (75-5759/4996 rebuilt & fitted with 190bhp Lycoming O-435-11 for Rep of China in 1947) ex 42-16724/16845
E75 (PT-13D)	75-5009/5158	42-16846/16995	150 a/c (Bu 60887/61036 ntu)
E75 (N2S-5)	75-5159/5219	61037/61097	61 a/c ex 42-16996/17056
E75 (PT-13D)	75-5220/5226	42-17057/17063	7 a/c (Bu 61098/61104 ntu)
E75 (N2S-5)	75-5227/5242	61105/61120	16 a/c ex 42-17064/17079
E75 (PT-13D)	75-5243/5258	42-17080/17095	16 a/c (Bu 61121/61136 ntu)
E75 (N2S-5)	75-5259	61137	1 a/c ex 42-17096
E75 (PT-13D)	75-5260/5264	42-17097/17101	5 a/c (Bu 61138/61142 ntu)
E75 (N2S-5)	75-5265/5277	61143/61155	13 a/c ex 42-17102/17114
E75 (PT-13D)	75-5278/5297	42-17115/17134	20 a/c (Bu 61156/61175 ntu)
E75 (N2S-5)	75-5298/5312	61176/61190	15 a/c ex 42-17135/17149
E75 (PT-13D)	75-5313/5345	42-17150/17182	33 a/c (Bu 61191/61223 ntu)
E75 (N2S-5)	75-5346	61224	1 a/c ex 42-17183
E75 (PT-13D)	75-5347/5353	42-17184/17190	7 a/c (Bu 61225/61231 ntu)
E75 (N2S-5)	75-5354/5362	61232/61240	9 a/c ex 42-17191/17199
E75 (PT-13D)	75-5363/5382	42-17200/17219	20 a/c (Bu 61241/61260 ntu)
E75 (N2S-5)	75-5383/5389	61261/61267	7 a/c ex 42-17220/17226
E75 (PT-13D)	75-5390/6026	42-17227/17863	637 a/c (Bu 61268/61904 ntu)
E75 (PT-13D)	75-6027/6408	42-17864/18245	382 a/c cancelled
B75N1 (N2S-3)	75-6409/6608	05235/05434	200 a/c
B75N1 (N2S-3)	75-6609/7608	07005/08004	1000 a/c
B75N1 (N2S-3)	75-7609/8058	37988/38437	450 a/c
E75 (N2S-5)	75-8059/8231	38438/38610	173 a/c ex 42-109026/109198
E75 (N2S-5)	75-8232/8731	43138/43637	500 a/c ex 42-109199/109698
E75 (N2S-5)	75-8732/8808	52550/52626	77 a/c ex 42-109699/109775
A76B4	76-074/078		5 a/c to Venezuela
A76C3/B76C3	76-014/028		15 a/c to Brazil as armed trainers with 420bhp Wright R-975E-3s
A76C3/B76C3	76-029/043		15 a/c to Brazil, with Fairchild K-3B aerial cameras
76D1	76-001/010		10 a/c for Argentine Navy, 320hp Wasp Jr.
76D1	76-011/013		3 a/c for Philippines
76D1	76-044/049		6 a/c for Argentine Navy
76D3	76-050/055		6 armed trainers for Philippines with 1 mg & camera
76D3	76-056/073		18 armed trainers for Philippines with 1 mg/no camera
76B4	76-074/78		5 a/c to Venezuelan Air Force
80	80-001		420bhp 'Wasp' engine
81	81-001		Amphibian. Sold to Mexican Govt in August 1933
X-85 (XOSS-1)	85-000	1052	US Navy Scout-Observation amphibian. Delv'd August 1938

Anyone wishing to begin a restoration project, or simply who has a more general interest in Stearmans, should join the SRA Membership, which is contactable at P.O. Box 10663, Rockville, Maryland 20849-0663. USA. Stearman restoration is well nigh impossible without the support and expertise of Dusters & Sprayers Supply Inc., of PO Box 766, Chickasha, Oklahoma 73018, the world's foremost suppliers of parts for rebuilds.